Lucy Jackson for Nusu Nusu Productions in association
with Neil McPherson for the Finborough Theatre presents

As part of the New Writing at the Finborough Theatre
Season November 2011 to January 2012

The World Premiere

FANTA ORANGE

by Sally Woodcock

FINBOROUGH | THEATRE

First performance at the Finborough Theatre, Tuesday, 1 November 2011

Fanta Orange

by Sally Woodcock

Cast in order of appearance

Regina	**Kehinde Fadipe**
Ronnie	**Jessica Ellerby**
Roger	**Jay Villiers**

The action takes place in and around Roger's farmhouse in Kenya, East Africa, the present.

The performance lasts approximately two hours.

There will be one interval of fifteen minutes.

Director	**Gareth Machin**
Designer	**Alex Marker**
Lighting Designer	**Neill Brinkworth**
Sound Designer	**Tom Gibbons**
Dialect Coach	**Kay Welch**
Stage Manager	**Louise Buckton**
Producer	**Lucy Jackson**
Casting Director	**Hayley Kaimakliotis**
Assistant Director	**Ola Ince**
Production Assistant	**George Ransley**

Our patrons are respectfully reminded that, in this intimate theatre, any noise such as rustling programmes, talking or the ringing of mobile phones may distract the actors and your fellow audience-members.

Jessica Ellerby | Ronnie
At the Finborough Theatre, Jessica appeared in
Oohrah! (2009).
Trained at Bristol Old Vic Theatre School.
Theatre includes *Dreamboats and Petticoats*
(Playhouse Theatre), *Curvature, Word:Play 2*
(Theatre503), *Captain of the School Football Team*
(Latitude Festival and Theatre503), *Dick Whittington*
(Theatre Chipping Norton), *Triptych* (Southwark Playhouse), *Push Up*
(Rosemary Branch Theatre) and *My Name Is Alice* (Edinburgh Festival).
Film includes *Magpie, Hollow, Get Him To The Greek* and *The Sad Case*.
Television includes *EastEnders* and *The Bill*.

Kehinde Fadipe | Regina
At the Finborough Theatre, Kehinde appeared in
Hurried Steps (2009) and *And I And Silence* as part
of *Vibrant – An Anniversary Festival of Finborough
Playwrights* (2010).
Trained at the Royal Academy of Dramatic Art.
Theatre includes *Ruined* (Almeida Theatre) and
Auricular (Theatre503).
Workshops include *Houseboy* (Tiata Fahodzi), *Mephisto* (MJE
Productions) and *Eclipsed* (National Theatre Studio).
Television includes *Misfits* and *Body Farm*.
Short Film includes *Of Mary*.

Jay Villiers | Roger
Trained at Bristol Old Vic Theatre School.
Theatre includes *In Praise Of Love* (Theatre Royal,
Northampton), *A Midsummer Night's Dream,
Hamlet* and *Much Ado About Nothing* (The Tobacco
Factory), *Gone To Earth* (Shared Experience, Lyric
Hammersmith and Tour), *Barbarians, The Taming Of
The Shrew* and *Dead Funny* (Salisbury Playhouse),
Betrayal and *The Browning Version* (Bristol Old Vic), *Arcadia, Mansfield
Park* and *The Admirable Crichton* (Chichester Festival Theatre), *Six
Degrees Of Separation* (Crucible Theatre, Sheffield), *Hamlet, As You Like
It* and *Much Ado About Nothing* (Renaissance Theatre Company), *Ting
Tang Mine, Fathers And Sons* and *Six Characters In Search Of An Author*
(National Theatre) and *Richard III* (Royal Shakespeare Company).
Film includes *The Best Exotic Marigold Hotel, The Lady, Before The Rain,
Decameron* and *Henry V*.
Television includes *Extras, Absolute Power, Lewis, Heartbeat, Midsomer
Murders, Spooks, Silent Witness, The Government Inspector, Monsignor
Renard, McCallum, The Sculptress, Black Hearts In Battersea,
Rumpole, Lipstick On Your Collar, The Young Indiana Jones Chronicles*
and *Miss Marple*.

Sally Woodcock | Playwright
Sally was raised in Kenya and educated at Cambridge University, RADA and King's College, London. She has worked as a journalist, teacher and theatre practitioner, writing and producing comedies (*Wedding Belles* and *The Trouser Department*) on the fringes of Edinburgh (The Gilded Balloon, Hill Street Theatre), London (Jermyn Street Theatre, Bridewell Theatre) and New York (78th St Theatre Lab). She also co-founded the Horseshoe Theatre Company which produced play texts for public examination students at theatres in Cambridge. *Fanta Orange* is Sally's first full-length play and has been developed at RADA and the National Theatre Studio.

Gareth Machin | Director
Until recently, Gareth was Studio Associate at the National Theatre where he directed Caryl Churchill's *Three More Sleepless Nights* in the Lyttelton Theatre. He has just been appointed Artistic Director of Salisbury Playhouse. He was previously Artistic Director of Southwark Playhouse where his productions included Chris Chibnall's *Gaffer* and Arthur Miller's *The Archbishop's Ceiling*. As Associate Director at Bristol Old Vic, his productions included major revivals of *Who's Afraid of Virginia Woolf?* with Clare Higgins and Gerard Murphy, *Look Back in Anger* with Nick Moran, many new plays in the New Vic Studio and establishing the Basement Theatre as a regular lunchtime and late night producing venue. He also co-directed the site-specific epic *Up The Feeder Down the Mouth and Back Again* in Bristol Docks.

Alex Marker | Designer
Alex has been Resident Designer of the Finborough Theatre since 2002 where his designs have included *Charlie's Wake, Soldiers, Happy Family, Trelawny of the 'Wells', Hortensia and the Museum of Dreams, Albert's Boy, Lark Rise to Candleford, Red Night, The Representative, Eden's Empire, Little Madam, Plague Over England* and its West End transfer to the Duchess Theatre, *Hangover Square, Sons of York, Untitled, Painting A Wall, Death of Long Pig, Molière or The League of Hypocrites, Me and Juliet, Quality Street* and *Dream of the Dog* and its West End transfer to the Trafalgar Studios. He has also directed at the Finborough Theatre including a staged reading of Iain Finlay MacLeod's *Atman*, starring Jasper Britton and Alan Cox, as part of *Vibrant – An Anniversary Festival of Finborough Playwrights* (2010) and a sell-out revival of William Douglas Home's *Portraits* (2011).
Trained in Theatre Design at Wimbledon School of Art, he has designed over fifty productions including *Jus' Like That – An Evening with Tommy Cooper* (National Tour), *King Arthur* (Arcola Theatre), *The Schools' Theatre Festival* (The Young Vic), *Origin: Unknown* (Theatre Royal, Stratford East), *The Real McCoy – Reconnected* (Hackney Empire and Broadway Theatre, Catford), *My Real War 1914-?* (Trafalgar Studios and

National Tour), *The Viewing Room* (Arts Theatre), *Sweet Charity* (Theatre Royal, Drury Lane), *Oklahoma!* (New Wimbledon Theatre) and *Cooking With Elvis* (Lyceum Theatre, Crewe). His work has been extensively featured in exhibitions, most recently as part of the *Transformation and Revelation: UK Design for Performance* in Cardiff. He is also Director of the Questors Youth Theatre, the largest youth theatre in London.

Neill Brinkworth | Lighting Designer
At the Finborough Theatre, Neill was Lighting Designer for *Fair* and its West End transfer (2005), *The Gabriels* (2006), *Accolade* (2011) and *Blue Surge* (2011).
Lighting Designs include *In the Night Garden* (Minor, Rag Doll and BBC), *The Seagull* (Arcola Theatre), *Agamemnon* (Cambridge Arts Theatre), *Vincent River* (Old Vic Productions at the Trafalgar Studios), *Seven Pomegranate Seeds* (Oxford Playhouse), *Deptford Stories* (National Theatre at The Albany), *Strauss Gala* (Raymond Gubbay), *Six Men and A Poker Game* (Grid Iron), *A Square of Sky, In the Store Room* (The Kosh), *Cats, The Wedding Singer, Footloose* (Arts Educational Schools), *Spangleguts* and *The Tinder Box* (London Bubble), *A Streetcar Named Desire* and *Tales of Ovid* (Guildhall School of Music and Drama), *The Handsomest Drowned Man* (The Circus Space), *The Canterville Ghost* and *A Christmas Carol* (Southwark Playhouse), *Dido and Aeneas, Bridgetower* and *Jephthe* (English Touring Opera), *Ludd and Isis* (Royal Opera House) and *Maria Stuarda* (Opera North).
Neill has worked as an Associate Lighting Designer for the Royal Opera House, Opera North and the Menier Chocolate Factory. Neill has re-lit national and international tours for English Touring Theatre, Michael Clarke Dance Company, English Touring Opera and *The Vagina Monologues*.

Tom Gibbons | Sound Designer
Trained at the Central School of Speech and Drama. Sound Designs include *Disco Pigs* (TheYoung Vic), *Dead Heavy Fantastic* (Everyman Theatre, Liverpool), *Plenty* (Crucible Studio, Sheffield), *Encourage The Others* (Almeida Theatre), *Love Love Love* and *Wasted* (National Tour for Paines Plough), *Faith, Hope and Charity, The Hostage* and *Toad* (Southwark Playhouse), *Sold* (Theatre503), *The Chairs* (Ustinov Bath), *The Country, The Road To Mecca, The Roman Bath, 1936* and *The Shawl* (Arcola Theatre), *The Knowledge, Little Platoons, 50*

Ways To Leave Your Lover, *50 Ways To Leave Your Lover@Xmas*
and *Broken Space Season* (Bush Theatre), *Bagpuss*, *Everything
Must Go* and *Soho Streets* (Soho Theatre), *The Machine
Gunners* (Polka Theatre), *Terror Tales* (Hampstead Theatre
Studio), *Faustus* (Watford Palace and Tour), *FAT* (Oval House
Theatre and National Tour) and *Just Me Bell* (Graeae and Tour).
As Associate, Tom designed *The Aliens* (Bush Theatre). He is
Resident Sound Designer for the international physical theatre
company Parrot{in the}Tank.

Kay Welch | Dialect Coach
Trained at the Central School of Speech and Drama. Kay Welch
has been working as an Accent and Dialect Coach for the last
six years at several drama schools including Rose Bruford
College and the Arts Educational Schools. Recent theatre
includes *The Railway Children* (Waterloo Station) and *Kingdom
of Earth* (The Print Room).

Lucy Jackson | Producer
For the Finborough Theatre, Lucy has produced all of the
theatre's *Vibrant – A Festival of Finborough Playwrights* festivals
(2009, 2010 and 2011).
Other recent theatre includes *Amphibians*, nominated for
six OffWestEnd Awards (Offstage Theatre and Bridewell
Theatre), *Phillipa and Will are Now in a Relationship* and *The
Sexual Awakening of Peter Mayo* (Pleasance Edinburgh and
Theatre503) and *The 24 Hour Plays* for Old Vic New Voices
(The Old Vic), *The TS Eliot US/UK Exchange* (The Old Vic)
and *Time Warner Ignite 4*. She has produced at six Edinburgh
Festivals including this year *White Rabbit, Red Rabbit* (Volcano
Theatre) and *Thom Tuck Goes Straight-to-DVD* (Fosters
Edinburgh Comedy Award Nominee for Best Newcomer). She
is a Production Assistant for TEG Productions/Jeremy Meadow
Ltd, and General Manager for Tangram Theatre Company

Production Acknowledgements
Assistant Stage Manager **George Ransley**
Poster and Leaflet Design **Felix Trench**
Rehearsal Space **The Welsh Chapel**
Production Insurance **Israel Gordon and Co**
Set constructed at **Questors Theatre, Ealing**
Design Assistants **Henrietta Burton, Nathalie Parsons, Lucy Flach** and **Ellis McNorthey-Gibbs**

Thanks to:

DLKWLOWE

Natalie Parsons

Liorah Tchiprout

Philip Lindley

Rhian Morris

Zosia Stella-Sawicka

Jennie Yates

Questors Theatre

Sally Woodcock

FANTA ORANGE

OBERON BOOKS
LONDON

WWW.OBERONBOOKS.COM

First published in 2011 by Oberon Books Ltd

521 Caledonian Road, London N7 9RH

Tel: +44 (0) 20 7607 3637 / Fax: +44 (0) 20 7607 3629

e-mail: info@oberonbooks.com

www.oberonbooks.com

A catalogue record for this book is available from the British Library.

ISBN: 978-1-84943-196-5

E ISBN: 978-1-84943-544-4

Series: Oberon Modern Plays

Special thanks to Paul Sirett who first championed this play. Thank you also to Sebastian Born, Chris Campbell, Gareth Machin and the National Theatre Studio, and also to Sue Dunderdale at RADA, for enabling its development.

Characters

RONNIE
A white woman in her mid twenties.

ROGER
A white man in his mid forties.

REGINA
A black woman in her late teens/early twenties.

Note
The bold text indicates raised voice or emphasis.
The / mark indicates overlapping speech.

The story takes place in the present day in Kenya.

ACT ONE

PROLOGUE

*ROGER and RONNIE are seated at a bar, in shadow. Spotlight on
REGINA as SPIRIT.*

REGINA as SPIRIT: *(She waits for absolute quiet.)* See… He is
just meeting her for the first time. Do you see? He has
approached her – just now. It is the first time. Let us see. I
want to know everything which came to pass. Come with
me. Together we can go back. *(She moves in.)*

SCENE ONE

RONNIE sits at a bar. ROGER is there.

RONNIE: Geophagy.

ROGER: Geography?

RONNIE: **Geophagy.**

ROGER: Geology?

RONNIE: *Geophagy.*

ROGER: Geometry?

RONNIE: **GEOPH /AGY!**

ROGER: **CHRIST /MAN! KEEP YOUR KNICKERS ON!**
(Pause.)

RONNIE: I fully intend to. *(Beat.)*

ROGER: Gee-off-fah-jee. *(Beat.)* GEE-off-a-jee. *(Beat.)* Gee-
OFF-a-jee. / Gee-off- /AAA

RONNIE: **YES**! / *(Beat.)* You got there. Well done.

ROGER: What the hell is 'Geophagy'? *(Beat.)* Hey – hey – are
you making up this crap? To impress me? / If you want me
to buy you a –

RONNIE: **To impress you**? / Are you kidding?

17

ROGER: I was going to buy you a drink anyway – you don't have to go to / all these lengths –

RONNIE: **I have a drink.** / I have a drink. Thank you. *(Beat.)*

ROGER: OK. So what is Geophagy?

RONNIE: See if you can guess.

ROGER: Geophagy...OK. About earth or soil or something.

RONNIE: To do with soil, yes.

ROGER: 'Gee-O' – see? I'm very educated. I did Latin at school.

RONNIE: So did I. For A Level. Got an A as it happens. *(Beat.)*

ROGER: Brainy as well as beautiful, hey? Ach, brainy women – pain in the arse.

RONNIE: So why don't you go away? I'd really really like that.

ROGER: Because you're beautiful. If you were just brainy I'd be gone, trust me. Gone! You wouldn't see me for dust. Or earth. Or soil. *(Beat.)* I'm going just now. *(Beat.)* Just now. *(He stays.)* Geophagy. Ach: put me out of my misery: what is it? *(She does not respond.)* I was right: you just made it up, didn't you? To get some sort of fancy / grant –

RONNIE: **It's / the study of soil eating.** *(Beat.)*

ROGER: Soil – eating? *(Beat.)* Soil **eating**?

RONNIE: Yes.

ROGER: **You eat soil**? Suss man! That's sick, man! You are sick, man! **This woman eats soil** – James, take these bloody nuts away – / shit –

RONNIE: I don't eat / soil! –

ROGER: You / dirty bitch! *(Pause.)* Sorry. That was uncalled for. *(Pause.)*

RONNIE: If you must know, I'm conducting research for my thesis on the practice of earth ingestion among the peoples of Western Kenya: a practice found to meet dietary deficiencies in a number of minerals, including

18

phosphorus, potassium, magnesium, copper, zinc, manganese, and iron. *(Pause.)*

ROGER: Ah. *(Beat.)* Very good; very impressive. *(To himself.)* Another one of those, hey?

RONNIE: One of 'those' what?

ROGER: One of Those. You know. **Those.** *(Beat.)* Tho-o-o-o-se...

RONNIE: Ah! You mean another clueless white woman with her conscience-stricken hat on, come to deliver The African from famine, disease, earthquake, wind and fire – whilst secretly revelling in her ability to retreat to the nearest luxury lodge when the going gets tough. Or the dysentery kicks in. *(Beat.)*

ROGER: Yah. Pretty much.

RONNIE: Well – actually – no. Not another one of 'those'.

ROGER: You sure about that?

RONNIE: Look, piss off will you?

ROGER: I'm going just now. *(Pause. They both drink.)*

RONNIE: Tell me something?

ROGER: I'll try...

RONNIE: You're probably twenty, thirty years older than me –

ROGER: Whoa – I'm 45!

RONNIE: You look about 95.

ROGER: Hey, come on –

RONNIE: You've got so much sun damage you look like someone chucked a bowl of cornflakes at your face, your beer gut is –

ROGER: What beer gut?

RONNIE: – peering seductively over your Swinging Safari shorts –

ROGER: – What – no – that's not – my belt's too small –

RONNIE: – all you need is a pith helmet and you could be on the set of Dad's Army –

ROGER: – What's wrong with my shorts? –

RONNIE: – Let's face it, you're not exactly Tarzan, / are you.

ROGER: Hey! / Actually he's my twin brother.

RONNIE: Whilst I, as you astutely note, am beautiful. *(Beat.)*

ROGER: You're not bad.

RONNIE: And brainy. So don't you think you're somewhat out of your league? *(Beat.)*

ROGER: As it happens, I've gone off you a bit. Now I know you eat dirt.

RONNIE: I don't eat dirt!

ROGER: And now I'm looking a bit closer you're a bit – grubby. Suss man, look at your fingernails! Hey – get your filthy hands away from me! **Get this filthy woman off me!**

RONNIE: **Oh shut up!** *(Beat.)* Look. I haven't had a shower for a month so – yuh – I'm filthy and – yuh – I probably stink. So – yes – good – I hope it does put you off. Good.

ROGER: Good.

RONNIE: Good.

ROGER: Good.

RONNIE: So perhaps now you would care to leave me in peace. *(Beat.)* Till I return to my mud hut. To shit in a hole. *(Beat.)*

ROGER: Problem is, we both know you'd scrub up like a dream…

RONNIE: Problem is, I like being dirty.

ROGER: This is music to my ears.

RONNIE: Look, I have to tell you, the 'sugar daddy' thing isn't doing it for me, if that's what you / had in mind –

ROGER: **Sugar daddy?** / Ach – I'm just a kid, man! –

RONNIE: – and I don't need you to buy me drinks. I can buy my own. Because I have a fucking enormous trust fund.

ROGER: This is not making you any less attractive to me.

RONNIE: Well it's making you monumentally less attractive to me. *(Beat.)*

ROGER: So. I guess it's just a numbers game.

RONNIE: What is?

ROGER: A percentage situation.

RONNIE: In what sense?

ROGER: That puts me in with a chance.

RONNIE: I'm not getting your maths.

ROGER: Well I'm the only guy here.

RONNIE: No you're not.

ROGER: Ah – there's another geophagy-ologist?

RONNIE: No – there's dozens.

ROGER: Dozens of geophagy-ologists? Shit, man! Where?

RONNIE: Dozens of men. There's James for a start.

ROGER: Who's James?

RONNIE: James – who mixed my drink. He's way better looking than you, a lot more polite, and probably a lot better hung.

ROGER: **You're after James**?

RONNIE: I might be.

ROGER: Ach, you people… You're after James!

RONNIE: I hadn't thought about it. Till now. As it happens he's not really my type.

ROGER: Not your type? Why not?

RONNIE: Because he's black.

ROGER: Because he's black?

RONNIE: Yuh. Mainly. I think so.

ROGER: You admit: you won't sleep with James because he's black!

RONNIE: Yeah…pretty much.

ROGER: You're not attracted to black men.

RONNIE: No, not generally.

ROGER: So – I'm in! You see, I'm the only white bugger here.

RONNIE: I'm probably not his type either.

ROGER: What's wrong with black men?

RONNIE: What sort of a question is that? Nothing's 'wrong' with black men. Like I said, I'm just not generally drawn to black men sexually. Or fat men. Or bald men. Not mad on ageing Kenya cowboys either – so that's you out. *(Beat.)* There are exceptions of course.

ROGER: Are there?

RONNIE: Last man I slept with. He was black.

ROGER: Jesus, don't tell me this.

RONNIE: Well I say black… More – chestnut, really… A deep, / dark –

ROGER: Did he eat dirt?

RONNIE: I doubt it. Likes a good rib-eye steak though. Very rare.

ROGER: Ah!

RONNIE: Ah. Yes. **That** sort of black man.

ROGER: Ah! Not a dirt-eater.

RONNIE: No no. Rib-eye steak-eater. Worships Kipling. Loves his Biggles. Knows the form. *(Beat.)*

ROGER: You know: you're more racist than me.

RONNIE: I'm not actually competing.

ROGER: That comment about James being 'well-hung'. That's cheap. It's stereotyping.

RONNIE: Handy way to irritate wanky white men though. *(Beat.)*

ROGER: So why your fancy Biggles-lover and not the delightful James here?

RONNIE: Chemistry, I guess.

ROGER: Chemistry. *(Beat.)* Not Chemophagy?

RONNIE: **Piss off**. Look, I live, eat and sleep among an increasingly rootless community so malnourished they resort to eating dirt to fill their tummies and, in so doing, make themselves vulnerable to all manner of hideous debilitating diseases. I'm not doing any harm and I may actually be doing some good. So does it really make me such a hypocritical racist if I prefer not to sleep with a category of male-kind which doesn't happen to float my boat? I don't have to sleep with anyone out of some weird post-imperial guilt. I sleep with people for all sorts of reasons: curiosity, boredom, drunken abandon, good old fashioned lust… But guilt? Nah. Not so much. *(Beat.)*

ROGER: You're something else.

RONNIE: You're not.

ROGER: James! Another enormous vodka for this dirt-eating female.

RONNIE: I don't want another drink.

ROGER: What do you want?

RONNIE: I want to use your shower. *(Beat.)*

ROGER: Mind if I join you?

RONNIE: It's your shower. Do what you like. *(Blackout.)*

REGINA as SPIRIT appears from the shadows.

REGINA as SPIRIT: So fast! So fast… *(She strikes the scene, making eye contact with the audience as she does so and beckoning them 'in' to the next scene.)*

SCENE TWO

RONNIE and ROGER are in bed. REGINA as SPIRIT is in shadow. They do not see her.

ROGER: I think I'm in love you –

RONNIE: Who was the last person **you** slept with? –

ROGER: Will you marry me?

RONNIE: Who was the last person you slept with?

ROGER: What's your name again?

RONNIE: Ronnie. I told you, now you / tell me –

ROGER: **Ronnie**? Like Ronnie Corbett? / Ronnie Barker?

RONNIE: Who was the / last person you slept with?

ROGER: Ronnie will you marry me?

RONNIE: We should have used a condom. Now I'm going to die of AIDS. **Who was the last person you / slept with?**

ROGER: **Ronnie / will you marry me?** *(Beat.)*

RONNIE: I can't believe we never used a condom! I'm in Africa – what was I thinking?

ROGER: I love you. I've never met anyone like you.

RONNIE: I don't even know your name.

ROGER: Come and live with me on my farm. You'll love my farm.

RONNIE: What did you say your name was?

ROGER: I didn't.

RONNIE: Well, what is it?

ROGER: Roger. *(Beat.)*

RONNIE: Oh God – you're bound to have AIDS.

ROGER: I haven't got AIDS.

RONNIE: Who was the last person you slept with? *(Beat.)*

ROGER: My house girl.

RONNIE: Your house girl? Shit! Is she black?

ROGER: Of course she's black.

RONNIE: That's it – I'm dead.

ROGER: I told you you were racist.

RONNIE: You're kidding – you're 45, you live in Africa, you sleep with Africans – and you don't use condoms – how can you **not** be HIV-positive?

ROGER: I'm not. I was tested. Just last week in fact. And I don't sleep with Africans. *(Beat.)* But I am 45.

RONNIE: But you slept with your house girl.

ROGER: Yes. I slept with my house girl.

RONNIE: Is this just some stupid tit for tat?

ROGER: No. It's not.

RONNIE: Do you sleep with her often?

ROGER: No I slept with her once.

RONNIE: Will you sleep with her again?

ROGER: *(Beat.)* No.

RONNIE: Why?

ROGER: Because she's HIV-positive. *(Pause.)*

RONNIE: So how come you're not?

ROGER: I got lucky.

RONNIE: You got away with it.

ROGER: I got away with it. *(Beat.)*

RONNIE: How do you know **I'm** not?

ROGER: What?

RONNIE: HIV-positive.

ROGER: I don't. *(Beat.)* Are you?

RONNIE: No.

ROGER: How do you know?

RONNIE: Because I use condoms.

ROGER: No you don't.

RONNIE: Well I do usually.

ROGER: But not always. *(Beat.)*

RONNIE: No. *(Beat.)* Not always. Why did on earth did you sleep with your house girl?

ROGER: Why on earth not?

RONNIE: No. Really. *(Beat.)*

ROGER: Because I – I – felt sorry for her.

RONNIE: You felt sorry for her?

ROGER: Yes. *(He is unsettled.)*

RONNIE: That's patronising. And racist. **That's** racist.

ROGER: Is it?

RONNIE: Yes. Why did you feel sorry / for her?

ROGER: Did you / use a condom with your black man?

RONNIE: No. Why did you feel sorry / for her?

ROGER: Because / she was scared shitless. Did you say 'no'?

RONNIE: Yes. Scared shitless of what?

ROGER: Men. Did you say **'no'**?

RONNIE: Men?

ROGER: Yes.

RONNIE: White men?

ROGER: All men. But especially white men.

RONNIE: Why?

ROGER: Because she was raped. *(Beat.)* Did you say **no**?

RONNIE: Yes. By a white man?

ROGER: By a bunch.

RONNIE: A bunch? You mean – gang raped?

ROGER: Yes.

RONNIE: My God. By white men?

ROGER: British Army.

RONNIE: British Army? What all of them?

ROGER: No! Four. Five. Half a dozen, maybe. There's a base in town.

RONNIE: Where? When? I mean, how do you know?

ROGER: I found her. Just after it happened. Half-conscious. In a heap.

RONNIE: Shit.

ROGER: Yes. Shit.

RONNIE: When?

ROGER: New year's day. Early hours of the morning. I was on my way home from a piss-up. Bastards drove past me in their joy-mobile, drunk as skunks. Bhang-ied to the eyeballs. Then I saw her. Not far behind them. In a ditch. Crawling along. In tatters. So I picked her up. Took her home. *(Beat.)*

RONNIE: And slept with her.

ROGER: No – not then, man, no way: Christ, who d'you think I – ? No: she was a mess. A mess. She needed urgent medical attention. I had to take her to the hospital, get her…sorted out. No no. *(Beat.)* It was later – when she ran away.

RONNIE: Ran away? From what?

ROGER: Ach. Bunch of junglies in her village wanted to cut her up.

RONNIE: Cut her up?

ROGER: Circumcise her.

RONNIE: **Ouch**. But – why?

ROGER: Christ only knows. They'd branded her a whore or something. / Because she –

RONNIE: **A whore**? / Because she was raped?

ROGER: Something like that. Because she / had this kid –

RONNIE: How could she / possibly be a blamed for that?
(Beat.)

ROGER: Ach, these people are rough, man – / don't kid
yourself.

RONNIE: / So she ran to you. / For protection.

ROGER: She needed a job. And a home. So I gave her a job.
In my house.

RONNIE: And then you slept with her.

ROGER: Once. It seemed like a good idea – I don't know – I
thought it might help.

RONNIE: How kind.

ROGER: Ach, it wasn't like that. She was in a hell of a state.
I just had this feeling – thought it might make it better
for her to…sleep…with someone – a white man even – a
white man especially – just once – that wasn't bad sex. Just
– just – normal – decent sex.

RONNIE: Love-making.

ROGER: If you like. *(Beat.)* But on her terms. I wanted to – to
– to –

RONNIE: Comfort her.

ROGER: Yes. More or less. So I offered. *(Beat.)*

RONNIE: And she accepted.

ROGER: Yes. *(Beat.)*

RONNIE: But she has AIDS.

ROGER: She's HIV-positive.

RONNIE: Did you know?

ROGER: No. Not at the time. I took a risk.

RONNIE: You didn't use a condom?

ROGER: No.

RONNIE: Why?

ROGER: Because I needed to be – I don't know –

RONNIE: Sympathetic.

ROGER: Yes. Or something. A condom would have, you know –

RONNIE: Ruined it. Like she was infected – broken the spell.

ROGER: Yes, sort of. Yes.

RONNIE: But she is infected?

ROGER: Yes.

RONNIE: From the rapes.

ROGER: I assume.

RONNIE: Did she get herself tested?

ROGER: No no. Not at the time. But I took her recently. *(Beat.)* Just last week in fact.

RONNIE: Why? If she's –

ROGER: Because she's pregnant.

RONNIE: Pregnant? Oh shit. *(Beat.)* Oh my God how awful: by the – from the – from the – ohmygod from the – ? *(She looks at him, searchingly. Spotlight on REGINA as SPIRIT who also searches ROGER for eye contact; he does not see her but he is uneasy.)* Yes. *(Pause.)* From the rapes. *(Beat.)*

ROGER: She needed proper care – you see – medical care – and the baby – if you play it right, if you play it right, you can stop transmission. To the baby. Caesarian. ARVs. No breast feeding, that kind of stuff, all kinds of stuff you can do to prevent –

RONNIE: Yes I will marry you.

ROGER: *(Beat.)* Too late, I've changed my mind.

RONNIE: Too late, I've accepted.

ROGER: You could be a pest.

RONNIE: I love you.

ROGER: What about your dirt-eating?

RONNIE: I don't eat dirt.

ROGER: What about your thesis?

RONNIE: A few more weeks. Then I'll come. To your farm.

ROGER: You didn't use a jonny with your black man.

RONNIE: No.

ROGER: Maybe you're infected.

RONNIE: I'm fine. He was rich. He was in London.

ROGER: So was Freddie Mercury.

RONNIE: You risked it for your house girl. Are you prepared to risk it for me?

ROGER: I just did.

RONNIE: Will you marry me?

ROGER: Yes. *(Beat.)* Do you want kids?

RONNIE: No. *(Beat.)* NO. This country's way too overpopulated /already.

ROGER: **Yes** / you do.

RONNIE: Yes I do.

ROGER: A bunch.

RONNIE: A big bunch.

ROGER: Little Africans.

RONNIE: Yes. Little Africans.

ROGER: Little white Africans.

RONNIE: Don't say that.

ROGER: Why not?

RONNIE: It makes me uncomfortable.

ROGER: I just did.

Blackout. Spotlight on REGINA as SPIRIT.

REGINA as SPIRIT: Yes. It was the first day of the year. Very early in the morning. I was walking just near the dirt road from that ridge. I saw the vehicle approach: big like a matatu. It was full of wazungu soldiers. The vehicle it stopped and one man, he got out. I could hear some other wazungu men laughing and shouting inside the car. The man came over the field to me; he said to me, 'Jambo, pretty lady.' I said, 'Jambo.' I was shy but I was not afraid – I even laughed – I thought he wanted to ask me the directions.

She strikes the scene.

SCENE THREE

ROGER sits at a small table on his verandah, finishing his breakfast. REGINA as SPIRIT 'shows' the scene.

REGINA as SPIRIT: Now he has returned. I heard his car return late in the night – it is a far journey from that lake. After that journey always he was so hungry. Come: you will see. *(She clears his plate.)*

ROGER: Asante, Regina: I've missed your cooking – that crap they've been feeding me at the lodge, eggs like rubber balls, you could play tennis with them. *(REGINA giggles. They share a moment. She goes to leave.)* Regina, wait – I – I – *(Beat.)* I – er – I – Regina, I'm getting married. *(She freezes. Then continues.)*

REGINA: You are getting married, Bwana?

ROGER: Yes. Yes. I am.

REGINA: Who is she?

ROGER: Girl I met fishing, actually.

REGINA: Fishing. Just now.

ROGER: Yes. Just now. At the weekend. *(Beat.)* Her name's Ronnie.

REGINA: Her name is Ronnie.

ROGER: Yes.

REGINA: It is a man's name.

ROGER: Short for Veronica.

REGINA: Her name is Veronica.

ROGER: Yes. Ronnie.

REGINA: You met her just now.

ROGER: Just now. Yes.

REGINA: So fast?

ROGER: Yes, it's a bit sudden I know. All these years on my own and – well – but I think you'll like her, Regina.

REGINA: She is mzungu?

ROGER: Yes. Yes. Mzungu. British. Well – English.

REGINA: *(Turning.)* So when is she coming to stay in this house?

ROGER: Any time. Soon. She's just finishing her studies. She studies the Luo, you know: what they eat. And so on. *(Beat.)* Before the rains I hope.

REGINA: And what about me?

ROGER: What about you?

REGINA: What will happen now to me? / To –

ROGER: Regina, / don't worry. Don't worry about any of – of – it'll be alright. I'll take care of – of you – of all of it – it'll all work out. One way or another. Trust me.

REGINA: Does she – Veronica – does she know –

ROGER: – No – no no no. No. Well, yes. Yes. No.

REGINA: Yes? Or No?

ROGER: Well. Yes and no.

REGINA: Yes and no?

ROGER: No. Yes. No. Well, not that it's, I mean, not about… about…but she knows, she does know, about – about, you know –

REGINA: What does she know?

ROGER: Everything. *(Beat.)* Almost.

REGINA: Does she know that you were together with me. / That we –

ROGER: **Yes.** / I told her all that. Straight away I told her all that. She knows.

REGINA: And that now I am expecting a child?

ROGER: Yes. Absolutely. Yes. She knows that too. *(Beat.)*

REGINA: Does she know that I was attacked by those British.

ROGER: Yes yes yes. She does. *(She looks at him intently.)*

REGINA: What does she not know?

ROGER: Well. In fact, Regina, she doesn't know – what she doesn't know – is – I think she thinks the toto, this toto, the baby, the – pregnancy – this pregnancy – is – well, I didn't mention any dates as such, and I think she…she, well, she, well I think she thought, she thinks, I think she put two and two together. And – sort of – made five. *(Beat.)*

REGINA: She cannot count.

ROGER: No.

REGINA: She knows that just now I am expecting a child.

ROGER: Yes.

REGINA: But she believes that the child in my stomach just now is –

ROGER: Yes.

REGINA: – the result of British attacks.

ROGER: Yes.

REGINA: But there was another child.

ROGER: Yes yes, I know all that. I know all that. But she doesn't need to know all that –

REGINA: You not tell her about my first child –

ROGER: No – well – not exactly –

REGINA: You did not tell her about the British child.

ROGER: – Regina, I told her everything. I told you. She jumped to conclusions.

REGINA: But you did not correct?

ROGER: No. Well – yes, but – well, no. I – I thought it best, since she – I mean, I didn't plan it that way – but in actual fact, it's probably best for her – well, and for you in many ways – for all of us – if she doesn't know that you and me are having a…if…if I – if you – if she doesn't know. *(Beat.)* So let's keep it that way, Regina. Please. We need to keep it that way. Both of us. *(Beat.)* Do you understand?

REGINA: *(Beat.)* Sielewi, Bwana.

ROGER: *(Impatient.)* No. Well you don't need to, Regina. You don't need to understand. Really. But let's just say – let's just say – it's our secret, Regina. Our secret. Yours and mine. *(Beat.)* That's all you need to know. *(Beat.)* Sawa?

REGINA: Sawa, Bwana. *(He hovers awkwardly, then exits. Light changes.)*

REGINA as SPIRIT: How could I understand? Did you see? All the time he said 'yes' and he said 'no'. At the same time. This was not a clear way to speak.

But this one matter – it was clear: I must keep this secret. This was clear for me. You see, in my mother tongue, Gikuyu, the mother she is called 'Mutumia'. This word it means the person who keeps the family secrets. So now for me it was the same. In this family I was Mutumia. This woman did not know I was to be mother to this man's child. It was my duty to keep this secret.

Let me tell you one more secret. In the eyes of Gikuyu people, she who is mother to a man's first born child, she is called his Number One Wife. So, you see, for this man I was Number One Wife. That was my secret. *(Enter ROGER.)*

ROGER: – Regina – uh – one more thing, while I remember… *(Beat.)*

REGINA: Yes Bwana?

ROGER: I'd like you to speak Swahili to Ronnie. To – er – Memsahib. If you don't mind.

REGINA: To speak with her in Swahili?

ROGER: Yes.

REGINA: Only in Kiswahili?

ROGER: Yes. Yes I think so.

REGINA: Kwa nini, Bwana?

ROGER: Because…um…well, it will help her…learn…you know…help her…speak. I think. And it will just keep things – between you – the two of you – more…less… messy.

REGINA: But my English – it is very fine – / even since I –

ROGER: Yes. Yes, / I know, your English is good, it's very fine. But – but – I – I – I just think it will be – better this way. Easier.

REGINA: It will be easier?

ROGER: Yes. I think so. For – for – well everyone, really. Naelewa? *(Beat.)* **Regina?**

REGINA: Naelewa, Bwana.

ROGER: Sawa sawa. *(Beat.)* Sawa sawa. *(He exits.)*

REGINA as SPIRIT: My tongue, you see, it was tied. My secrets were my only power.

She finishes striking the old and setting the new scene.

SCENE FOUR

We hear ROGER and RONNIE chatting offstage. REGINA as SPIRIT is attaching a baby 'bump' to herself as she speaks.

REGINA as SPIRIT: Now we can see the first arrival of Veronica in this house. Also it was my first time to see her. It was not a good day for me. *(She stands to attention at the front door as they arrive laden with baggage.)*

ROGER: Ah, Regina –

RONNIE: Regina! This is Regina! I've heard so much about you, Regina. Habari?

REGINA: Mzuri.

RONNIE: Good! Good! Mzuri! And habari ya – ? How is – ? How do you say 'baby'?

ROGER: Kitoto.

RONNIE: Habari kitoto, Regina? *(Pause.)*

ROGER: Regina, Memsahib nasema –

REGINA: Sijui. *(Beat.)*

ROGER: She doesn't know –

RONNIE: No. No. I know. *(She holds both REGINA's hands. In Swahili.)* Sorry for your troubles, Regina. *(Pause. REGINA removes her hands. Awkward. Pause.)*

ROGER: *(In Swahili.)* Haya, Regina, tell Boniface to get the bags from the car.

REGINA: Sawa, Bwana.

REGINA exits, returning as SPIRIT to observe.

RONNIE: God, she must hate me.

ROGER: Welcome home, my beauty…

RONNIE: And no wonder. The poor poor girl…

ROGER: She's fine, come here.

RONNIE: Appalling when you think about it. I mean, the poor, poor thing.

ROGER: Oh forgodsake – come here –

RONNIE: She must hate me! She's only –

ROGER: She doesn't hate you – Look, they're not like that – they don't –

RONNIE: 'They'? Who's 'they'?

ROGER: They don't feel that sort of –

RONNIE: Of course 'they' do! She's jealous: she had you all to herself and now –

ROGER: Ach, Ronnie, don't be a pain in the arse – here – / pack it in – *(He scoops her up and carries her over the threshold.)*

RONNIE: Aaaaaaargh! / What are you doing?

ROGER: *(He kisses her.)* Welcome home. And for chrissakes shut up.

RONNIE: Oh-my-god, look at your house – it's so sweet – it's really sweet – like a time warp – the fireplace – is that a buffalo head – oh-my-god the view – *(She struggles down.)*

ROGER: Yah well housekeeping's not my strong point but the view takes some beating –

RONNIE: Mount Kenya. Oh wow, oh my God. It's like someone's drawn it –   on the sky – with a – it's – oh Rog, it's to die for…

ROGER: It's where I'm going to die. Inshallah.

RONNIE: Wow.

ROGER: Not bad, hey?

RONNIE: It's heaven. *(Pause.)* Will you marry me?

ROGER: Ach, why not? Since you're here.

RONNIE: Oh, Rog – this is all so weird – bizarre – I can't believe it –

ROGER: Let's get beers – where's Boniface? Beer or vodka? We need to celebrate.

RONNIE: No. Neither. No.

ROGER: What d'you mean 'no'? This calls for a major piss up. / Boniface!

RONNIE: No. Roger / – I'm pregnant. *(Pause.)*

ROGER: Huh?

RONNIE: You heard.

ROGER: What? *(Beat.)* Already?

RONNIE: Yes. I think so.

ROGER: What – but – why? – I mean: How?

RONNIE: How? The night we met –

ROGER: Yah – but only – we only –

RONNIE: That's all it takes. Apparently.

ROGER: Jesus. *(Pause.)* I thought you were – I thought you /
were…

RONNIE: You / thought wrong.

ROGER: Right. *(Beat.)*

RONNIE: I was living dangerously. *(Beat.)*

ROGER: Right. *(Beat.)* So was I, it seems.

RONNIE: We both were. *(Beat.)* It takes two.

ROGER: Yes. *(Beat.)* I know that. *(Pause.)*

RONNIE: 'A little white African?'

ROGER: Right. A little white African. *(Pause.)*

RONNIE: But – but it's good, Rog… Isn't it? It's good news –
isn't it? It's – it's – Roger *(Beat.)* Are you happy?

ROGER: Happy? Happy. Am I happy? Am I happy. *(Beat.)*
Jesus Christ. I mean: Yes. Yes. Christ – but – OK – why
not? What we waiting for? Yes! Yes I'm happy! Are you?

RONNIE: Me? Yes – I think so! Yes! Bricking it a bit but – well,
a lot – but – yes – over the moon! I think… *(Beat.)* You
don't sound sure.

ROGER: Sure? Don't I? Don't sound sure. *(Beat.)* You know
what, Ronnie? I am sure. I am sure. Bloody right I am!
Hey – hey, Ron – this – this – this calls for a – for a –
for a major piss up! Major piss up! Big time! Boniface!
Boniface! Lete pombe – no – no – champagne! Mimi ni
Baba! Mimi ni Baba! I'm going to be a Daddy! I'm going
to be a fucking Daddy! **Boniface!** *(He exits.)*

RONNIE. *(Watching him go.)* Yes… Going to be a Daddy. And
I'm…oh God. Look at the mountain. *(Beat.)* Snow. On top.
In Africa snow: white snow on…white…in…in…oh God
– as if, as if. *(Beat.)* A little white African. *(Beat.)* A **white**?
No. I never thought but: Yes. A – a – a – yes. Why not?
Yes. It adds up – doesn't it? It all adds up. It can…add up.
It does. It adds up… *(Enter ROGER with two beers.)*

ROGER: Champagne's warm – nothing worse – like fizzy piss.
Let's kick off with beer.

RONNIE: Look at the mountain.

ROGER: Hey?

RONNIE: Rog – do you have any milk?

ROGER: Milk? No! I've got beers!

RONNIE: If you've got milk –

ROGER: Why the hell do you want milk? Come on, Ron! First drink in our new home, hey! We're having a – look! Here's to us! Here's to… It! Have a bloody beer!

RONNIE: I can't.

ROGER: Why the hell not?

RONNIE: It's bad for the –

ROGER: Oh Ronnie, forchrissakes – Kenyan kids are weaned on beer! We put it on our Weetabix! Start as we mean to go on, hey? Show the bugger who's boss.

RONNIE: Roger, I know who's boss and I don't want beer – I want milk.

ROGER: But we're celebrating!

RONNIE: I can celebrate with milk!

ROGER: Jesus Christ. So much for a piss up. Well, at least have a shot of / something –

RONNIE: Where's the fridge? / Where's the kitchen? I need to see the kitchen. I need some milk. *(She exits. He follows, muttering expletives. Lighting changes.)*

REGINA as SPIRIT enters. She is still.

REGINA as SPIRIT: 'Jambo, pretty lady,' he said. I even laughed. *(Beat.)* Then he said, 'Come here, pretty lady,' and very fast he grabbed me around my stomach and started to kiss my mouth. I tried to fight him, he tasted very bad, of beer and bhanghi smoke. He tasted very bad. I tried to fight him away. I was fighting. I tried to fight him away. *(Pause.)*

She strikes the scene.

SCENE FIVE

RONNIE and ROGER are in bed, fast asleep. REGINA is at the door with a tea tray.

REGINA as SPIRIT: It was my orders: every day early in the morning I was required to wake first in order to bring him some tea. *(REGINA knocks. Silence. She knocks again.)*

RONNIE: Hallo! *(Pause. She knocks again.)* Hallo! *(Pause.)* Rog, someone's at the door.

ROGER: Huh? What?

RONNIE: Someone at the door.

ROGER: What? *(Looks at clock.)* Oh, it's Regina. With the tea. Yes, yes, Regina – Come in! *(REGINA enters.)* Sawa, Regina, just leave it there – watcha uko – oh! *(There is stuff all over the table.)* Regina – *(He knocks over the clock.)* Oops – shit! Ronnie, there's nowhere –

RONNIE: Oh God, sorry – it's my stuff – I'll move it – oops, no, got no clothes –

ROGER: No, nor me – uh – hang on a minute… *(He tries to get out of bed wrapped in sheet but it is a fiasco, and he pulls the sheet off both of them.)* – Oh shit –

RONNIE: Oh God – *(She knocks over a glass of water.)* Oops!

ROGER: Oh bugger – *(They are both frantically covering themselves with sheets, pillows etc.)* Regina, just leave it on the floor – watcha chini – sawa – chini ni mzuri – *(REGINA puts tray on floor, picks up clock, puts it back, then clears RONNIE's knickers, bra etc. from the tea table. RONNIE covers herself with pillow etc. and tries to help.)*

RONNIE: Oh, Regina, please don't worry – Regina, pole – I'll do that – *(She slips on the spilt water, almost revealing herself.)* – **Ow!** Oops! Oh God…

ROGER: Regina, just leave it, leave it on the floor. *(She ignores him.)* Wacha hii! Weka chini! Forgodsake! Regina – **Just Go**! *(They lock eyes for a moment. REGINA leaves the tray on the table – now clear – and exits. Pause.)*

RONNIE: Oh God. *(Beat.)* It would be funny…if it wasn't so –
Oh God. Oh God. *(Beat.)*

ROGER: Morning, my lovely. *(She is pulling on a t-shirt under the bed clothes.)*

RONNIE: That was too weird. That was just too bloody weird.

ROGER: *(Peering under the bed clothes.)* Tea first – or sex?

RONNIE: *(Emerging.)* Did you do it in this bed? With her? Roger?

ROGER: No. *(He grimaces.)* Yes. *(Beat.)* Look. What does it matter?

RONNIE: Poor girl.

ROGER: It's not like that: I told you – they don't – it won't even / cross her –

RONNIE: Where's / the mountain? *(She opens the curtains.)*

ROGER: There she is. Clear as a bell.

RONNIE: Kirinyaga.

ROGER: Kikuyu name for it. *(He pulls on a kikoy and joins her.)*

RONNIE: Yes, I know. Place of darkness and light.

ROGER: 'Ira' means light.

RONNIE: Snow. On the equator.

ROGER: Did you know we have five out of six major terrestrial biosystems / in Kenya –

RONNIE: – all except / Arctic Tundra. I know.

ROGER: Course you do, my little Geophagy-ist.

RONNIE: Seems so odd somehow.

ROGER: What does?

RONNIE: Snow. On a mountain. In Africa. *(Pause.)* Odd. Somehow. Wrong. Almost. But right. Maybe… *(He goes to her.)*

ROGER: Sex before tea I think. *(Blackout.)*

Enter REGINA as SPIRIT to strike the scene.

REGINA as SPIRIT: That time, first he said 'no', and then he changed. Then he said 'yes'. Did you hear? *(Beat.)* Is it the same bed? Yes. It is the same bed.

SCENE SIX

REGINA is in her quarters stirring a pot. ROGER is there.

ROGER: Regina, have you taken your dawa this evening?

REGINA: I will take it.

ROGER: Make sure you do. It's dark in here. Can't see a bloody thing.

REGINA: Soon your eyes will start to work. *(She looks at him questioningly.)*

ROGER: Look. I just wanted to – look. Regina. Is this going to work? With you and the Memsahib? *(Beat.)* Tea in the morning. And so on. It's all a bit – tricky, isn't it? *(Beat.)*

REGINA: Si kitu, Bwana.

ROGER: Come on Regina, talk to me. *(Beat.)* Listen: would you rather not work – for me – in the house – now the Memsahib is…here? Is it going to be too –

REGINA: I have no place to go.

ROGER: No. No. I see what you mean. Your village, your shamba, / you don't want to –

REGINA: They will punish me – / they will cut me –

RONNIE: I know, Regina – / I know that.

REGINA: – they call me a / prostitute. A prostitute. They say the father of my child was / not –

ROGER: – Sh. / Sh. I know, Regina –

REGINA: The colour of that British, he was not –

ROGER: – it's OK. Regina. / It's OK. Shhhh. I know. *(He goes to hold her but stops himself.)* You can stay. I want you to stay. *(He almost touches her face.)*

REGINA: I want to stay here. With you. *(They are very close.)*

42

ROGER: Fine. That's fine. But Regina, I have to tell you: Memsahib is also expecting.

REGINA: *(Beat.)* She is expecting a child?

ROGER: Yes. A child.

REGINA: Veronica?

ROGER: Memsahib. Yes.

REGINA: So there will be two.

ROGER: Yes. Two.

REGINA: In this house.

ROGER: Yes. Yes. As I said.

REGINA: You are the father of both. At the same time.

ROGER: Well, yes. It does seem to be the case. *(Beat.)* Look, I'm sorry, Regina.

REGINA: You are sorry?

ROGER: Yes.

REGINA: Sorry – for what?

ROGER: Sorry – for you.

REGINA: Sorry – for me?

ROGER: Well yes – I mean, no – I mean –

REGINA: Yes? Or no?

ROGER: Yes – I said yes. Yes. But no – I mean…not sorry for you, I mean…sorry to you. I mean – just sorry. I don't know. *(Beat.)*

REGINA: You said –

ROGER: Look, Regina, it doesn't matter what I said. *(Beat.)* What matters, what I'm saying, what I'm trying to say is…is…what it is: Look – please – don't say – don't tell Ronnie…don't tell Memsahib…I told you, Regina. Please.

REGINA: About the child?

ROGER: Yes. *(Beat.)*

REGINA: Her child?

ROGER: Yes.

REGINA: It is a secret?

ROGER: Well, yes, for the time being.

REGINA: *(Beat.)* I am Mutumia.

ROGER: What?

REGINA: I can keep the secrets.

ROGER: Good, well done, Regina. Thank you. I knew you could. But I just thought you should know. I thought it was only…fair. *(Pause. He pulls away.)* But we'll have to change the system a bit. With tea. And so on. In future just leave the tray outside the door. In the morning. If you don't mind. I think. Regina. *(Beat.)* Sawa?

REGINA: Sawa, Bwana. *(He hovers, awkwardly.)* Lala Salama, Bwana.

ROGER: Yah. *(Beat.)* Lala Salama, Regina. Yah. *(He exits.)*

REGINA as SPIRIT: Do you see? He wanted me to stay close. But not close. Sorry and not sorry. Yes and no. At the same time. Many times it was so mixed. I could not see… But now…now, I begin to see. *(She strikes the scene.)*

SCENE SEVEN

ROGER is on verandah. Enter RONNIE, slightly pregnant, breathless, riding hat in hand. REGINA follows with a glass of milk and beer on a tray and bowl of nuts / crisps.

RONNIE: Guess what, Rog?

ROGER: What?

RONNIE: The most unbelievable thing!

ROGER: What?

RONNIE: I've just been at the far gate –

ROGER: Should you still be riding? *(He takes the beer.)*

ROGER: This woman was there, Rog – Samburu – selling fresh raw milk! Gallons of it. *(She takes the milk.)*

ROGER: They always do that. They come from far and wide.

RONNIE: Fresh milk! Straight from the cow! As though she'd read my mind.

ROGER: They come from all over, looking for takers. It's days old.

RONNIE: So I bought it – delicious!

ROGER: What, all of it? *(He is eating crisps.)*

RONNIE: Yes. 40 litres. *(REGINA, who has set bowls and cleared bottles, exits silently...)*

ROGER: Jesus wept! What do you want all that for?

RONNIE: It's fresh from the cow! Why don't we have cows?

ROGER: We do.

RONNIE: Where.

ROGER: On the ridge.

RONNIE: I thought that wasn't your land.

ROGER: It's not. But they're my cows.

RONNIE: What happens to the milk?

ROGER: You shouldn't drink it raw.

RONNIE: Why not? They all do.

ROGER: I wouldn't be so sure. What did you do with it all?

RONNIE: Drank as much as I could without bursting. Gave the rest to the lads.

ROGER: Ach, don't do that Ronnie.

RONNIE: Don't drink it?

ROGER: No – don't just dish out anything to the watu, willy nilly. I have a system.

RONNIE: Oh forgodsakes. They were thrilled!

ROGER: I bet they were. But the ones who missed out won't be. There'll be anarchy.

RONNIE: But it was so cheap.

ROGER: I don't care. I have a system. Don't mess it up.

RONNIE: *(Flirtatious.)* Are you being kali with me?

ROGER: I wouldn't dare. *(He pours another beer. REGINA as SPIRIT enters silently. They do not see her.)*

RONNIE: Look at the mountain.

ROGER: I've got to go to Nairobi tomorrow, Ron.

RONNIE: Why?

ROGER: See the bank. Grovel. Need to up my loan.

RONNIE: You have a loan?

ROGER: Ach, you don't know the half of it. Most of this bloody land is mortgaged to the hilt. Every year I swear I'll pay it off but some shauri comes along, back to square one.

RONNIE: What sort of shauri?

ROGER: Always something: drought, new bloody parasite, fuel price increase, elephants in the broccoli. It's giving me sleepless nights, I tell you.

RONNIE: Elephants in the broccoli!

ROGER: It's no joke, they massacred fifty acres.

RONNIE: Can't you pay it off?

ROGER: Don't you think I would if I could?

RONNIE: Poor boy. Poor headache. And there was I thinking you were a rich farmer.

ROGER: No you didn't.

RONNIE: No I didn't. *(Beat.)* I knew you were skint.

ROGER: And old. And 'out of my league'. According to you. So why exactly are you here? With me?

RONNIE: Good question. Very good question.

ROGER: Why then?

RONNIE: Honestly?

ROGER: Honestly.

RONNIE: Punishing myself. For past misdemeanours. You were the worst I could find.

ROGER: I half believe you.

RONNIE: You should. I'm half serious.

ROGER: Punishing me too now. A life bloody sentence.

RONNIE: Bloody right. When can we get married?

ROGER: Soon.

RONNIE: How soon?

ROGER: Soon soon.

RONNIE: Before the baby.

ROGER: Definite. *(Beat.)* Whose baby?

RONNIE: Our baby! *(She looks at him.)* Or Regina's. If you like. So much the better.

ROGER: She's due in two months.

RONNIE: I'm due in five.

ROGER: I need four. At least.

RONNIE: What for?

ROGER: To brace myself.

RONNIE: For a life sentence.

ROGER: Bloody right. *(Beat.)*

RONNIE: How much do you owe the bank?

ROGER: Too much.

RONNIE: So what sort of figure would make it all go away?

ROGER: Make what all go away?

RONNIE: Your poor man's headache, my darling, your sleepless nights.

ROGER: How much have you got?

RONNIE: Quite a lot as it happens.

ROGER: Miss Moneybags are we?

RONNIE: We might be... My family owns half of Shropshire you know – I'm an exceptionally good catch. Have you any idea?

ROGER: You can stick Shropshire up your arse.

RONNIE: Or I can stick it in Africa. On the farm. Our farm. If you can convince me it's a good use of my money – our money – once we're married. Whisper in my ear, go on – how much money would Bwana Kali need from the Shropshire money fairy? She may just be able to wave her magic wand and make all his wishes come true.

ROGER: The magic wand is my department, hey... But I'm interested in hearing more about this money fairy.

RONNIE: Whisper...

ROGER: Where exactly is this money tied up?

RONNIE: Whisper...

ROGER: I'm not whispering anything. I owe the bank twelve million shillings. And rising.

RONNIE: Which is about eighty grand. Look. That's not a problem, Rog – I'm serious. I can take care of that and still have plenty of change for ice creams. Listen, what's money for if not to take the stress out of our lives – and improve so many others'? Rog, I can't think of any better investment than a farm which employs 300 Africans, subsidises a canteen, health clinic and orphanage and plants ten indigenous trees every day. What you're doing here is totally amazing. I'm blown away. I'll be honest for a moment. I jumped into bed with you on – a whim.

ROGER: On the rebound from your fancy black man?

RONNIE: You were the next thing that came along. But maybe someone was looking after me – I love it here, what you're doing is incredible and I want to be part of it. Maybe I fell on my feet with you. I'm proud of you. You're my hero. I love you. *(Pause.)*

ROGER: Stop it. I like it.

RONNIE: Rog, let me pay off this silly debt. *(She goes to him.)*

ROGER: *(Intimately.)* You're amazing, you know that?

RONNIE: Yes, I know that. *(Pause.)* Will you let me, Rog?

ROGER: Ronnie, I can't. *(Pause.)* Can I?

RONNIE: Of course you can. Why can't you? Let me, Rog. Please. I want to.

ROGER: How much do you want to?

RONNIE: I really want to. I really really really want to…

ROGER: Ach, well – if you must, you must. *(They laugh. He kisses her.)*

REGINA as SPIRIT is watching them.

REGINA as SPIRIT: It is not a good idea. *(RONNIE breaks away from ROGER.)*

RONNIE: It **is** a good idea. *(Beat.)* I can right my wrong. I can give something back.

REGINA as SPIRIT: It is not a good idea. *(ROGER turns away from RONNIE.)*

ROGER: **It is a good idea**. *(Beat.)* People depend on me. I can save my farm.

ROGER and RONNIE are back to back.

REGINA as SPIRIT: It was not a good idea. These people felt it. In their bones. But they did not hear it in their ears. *(ROGER and RONNIE exit in opposite directions. REGINA as SPIRIT strikes the scene.)*

SCENE EIGHT

REGINA is on the verandah, setting the table for breakfast. Enter ROGER.

ROGER: Regina, I need some sandwiches. Haraka please. I'm going to Nairobi.

REGINA: Today, Bwana?

ROGER: Yes, just now. To the bank. Boniface is filling the car. I'm back tomorrow.

REGINA: Bwana, tomorrow I go to the clinic.

ROGER: Yes, yes, I know, Regina. Memsahib will take you.

REGINA: Veronica will take me?

ROGER: Yes. She's going herself. *(Pause.)* So you can show her the way, there's a good – a good – *(Enter RONNIE.)* Ah – Ron, can you take Regina to the clinic with you tomorrow?

RONNIE: Yes, yes, no problem. *(In Swahili.)* We'll go together, Regina. *(Pause. REGINA is silent.)*

ROGER: Sawa. Regina. Did you get a packet of ham?

RONNIE: No she didn't! I won't have that stuff in my fridge. Have you seen what's in it?

ROGER: Jesus. Well, cheese then, jibini, Regina. Na thermos ya chai, with proper milk – mziwa kwa duka. None of that Samburu shit.

RONNIE: 'That Samburu shit' is proper milk. That's exactly what it is.

ROGER: Tastes like crap. Good old-fashioned UHT, Regina, kwa carton. Asante.

REGINA: Sawa Bwana.

ROGER: Sawa Regina. *(They lock eyes for a moment. RONNIE sees. REGINA exits.)*

RONNIE: She does speak English, doesn't she?

ROGER: Hmm?

REGINA: She understands, doesn't she?

ROGER: Um, probably – a bit – not much – I don't really know.

RONNIE: She does. I can tell. *(Beat.)* You said she didn't.

ROGER: Did I?

RONNIE: You know you did. *(Beat.)* Rog, does she know?

ROGER: Know what?

RONNIE: About the baby.

ROGER: Which baby?

RONNIE: Our baby! Your baby! Obviously she knows about her own baby…

ROGER: I don't know.

RONNIE: Have you told her?

ROGER: No. *(Beat.)* Have you?

RONNIE: No. Not yet. *(Beat.)* But I think she knows. I'll tell her in the car. On the way to the clinic. We can do some sisterly bonding. *(She kisses him and exits.)*

ROGER: 'Sisterly bonding?' *(To himself.)* What the hell does that mean? *(Enter REGINA. He brushes past her.)* Jesus, Regina. I'm going to the bank. *(He exits. She is still.)*

REGINA as SPIRIT: I tried to fight him away. I was fighting. He tasted very bad. But then he was pushing me to the ground and lifting my skirt. I was making very much noise. I was screaming, 'Go away! Go away from me!' but then another man he came and he pushed my shoulders into the ground with his foot, it was so painful. I was screaming. And then that man he put his hand on my mouth, very hard. He pushed it so I could not breathe. *(Beat.)* I could not breathe. *(Pause. She strikes the scene.)*

SCENE NINE

RONNIE and REGINA are in the car.

RONNIE: Guess what, Regina? *(Pause.)* I'm pregnant too. *(Pause.)* Regina?

REGINA: Unasema, Memsahib?

RONNIE: I'm having a baby too, Regina. In December. *(Beat.)* There will be two babies. They can be friends. *(Beat.)* Naelewa?

REGINA: Sielewi.

RONNIE: Actually I think you do, Regina. I think you understand everything. I just…have a hunch. Anyway, even if you don't, even if I'm wrong…there's stuff I want to say anyway, stuff I'm going to say anyway. In English. Because, because – I need to – say it. I don't know why you won't speak to me, Regina. No, I do know why. Of course I do. And I don't blame you, God who can blame you, Regina? Certainly not me. Anyway, I thought you should know I'm having a baby too. We're both mothers-to-be: our babies will be almost twins! So we can help each other. If you like. If you'll let me. *(Beat.)* I'm having a check up at the clinic too, you see, so you'll find out sooner or later anyhow. Whether you understand me or not. *(Beat.)* And Regina, also – another thing – Look. I just want to say I know you – you – must have very – mixed feelings – towards your baby – and – God – I can't say I blame you, it being the result of such an unbelievably inhuman, brutal act, those – those savages... Look, Regina, it's none of my business, but whatever your – your gut feel – towards your baby – now – or after its born – or ever – really – the thing is...the thing is...I want you to know – I want you to know I know how it feels when...when your baby has the wrong...father. You see...I don't know how I will feel about my baby either. When I see it, hold it, smell it, hear its cry, see its...its skin. I don't know if I'll be able to...love it...as much as it deserves. You see, Regina – there was...another baby. An African baby. As it happens. At least, half African. Nusu nusu. It's father was African. He wasn't in Africa. But he was African. He was the father. Of this baby. But this baby was never born, you see. Regina. I...I...stopped it being born. Because I...because I...I didn't want it, Regina – at least, I thought, then, I didn't want it – so I...I...I got rid of it. *(Beat.)* But the thing is, I want it now, Regina, I want it now. But I can't have it. I can have this one – but I can't have that one. Not any more. Not any more. Because I...because I...And the thing is...I'm just not sure if this one...is the right one. You see. So, what I'm saying, what I'm trying to say, Regina is this: I have my pain too. It's pretty lame, perhaps, compared to yours. To the magnitude of your pain. Pretty lame. *(Beat.)* But I have my pain too. *(Pause.)* Regina, Naelewa? *(Pause.)*

REGINA: Naelewa. *(Beat.)* Mama.

RONNIE: I knew you did.

Exit RONNIE. REGINA strikes the scene.

SCENE TEN

ROGER is at a desk, battling with paperwork. REGINA as SPIRIT is there.
He meets and holds her eyes. Enter RONNIE in riding clothes. REGINA
takes up a broom and sweeps.

RONNIE: I have the most genius plan!

ROGER: Where have you been?

RONNIE: In town, talking about milk!

ROGER: Oh Christ, here we go.

RONNIE: Did you know they drink Fanta Orange?

ROGER: What? Who?

RONNIE: The orphans. At Nyumbani Orphanage – Fanta
Orange. They have it delivered – crates of the stuff – Fanta
bloody Orange – and we're subsidising it – it's a joke!

ROGER: It's the highlight of their day. They love it.

RONNIE: Of course they love it, it's a bright colour, it's full of
sugar and filthy E numbers, all highly addictive. Of course
they love it.

ROGER: Can we begrudge them this? When their parents have
died of AIDS?

RONNIE: They need milk!

ROGER: Oh Jesus.

RONNIE: Seriously, Rog, think about it. If we could supply
each of those kids with a glass of milk every day instead of
a bottle of…of toxic waste…they would thrive.

ROGER: Ronnie, milk is not going to cure AIDS.

RONNIE: It can't hurt! And many of them don't even have
AIDS – they're orphans because their parents have died
of it, not because they have it. Necessarily. 35% of babies

born to HIV-positive mothers contract the virus in utero, / the rest –

ROGER: **Don't you think I know that?**

RONNIE: Whoa… What's your problem?

ROGER: Milk's not straightforward. You have to think about packaging, refrigeration. It can't work.

RONNIE: It can, Rog, it can! We don't need to buy it from the dairies. Look, these tribeswomen are flocking here with it – gallons of it.

ROGER: That's because word's out there's some mad mzungu who chucks it back by the bucket-load!

RONNIE: But I've been turning them away in droves. I only buy it from my original lady, Mama Mziwa – I drink it every morning – religiously.

ROGER: Religion is a / dangerous thing –

RONNIE: I've stopped / dishing / it out to the staff because I didn't want to spoil your precious 'system' whatever that is. But half these women end up chucking it away because its gone off. It's a criminal waste, Rog.

ROGER: You can't give small children raw milk. / It's too risky.

RONNIE: I know: that's / exactly what this guy was saying at the dukas. *(Beat.)* Christian.

ROGER: Christian van Rensberg!

RONNIE: You know him?

ROGER: Big Girl's Blouse.

RONNIE: Whatever. Anyway he runs a dairy: Furaha Farm – 'Furaha' means happiness. They feed six local primary schools from the milk they process on site and still have a ton left over to sell – they've got a fantastic business going. 'Furaha' means / happiness!

ROGER: **I know / what 'furaha' means**. And I know Christian Van Rensberg – bloody blue-eyed milkman:

thinks he's Jesus Christ or something. Pain in the bloody arse.

RONNIE: Then he's a pain in the arse with the most unbelievable vision! They rear goats too, for children who can't tolerate cows' milk because their immune systems are compromised. Christian's even considering camels' milk –

ROGER: Oh for chrissakes –

RONNIE: I'm serious, some of these women bring camels' milk –

ROGER: I know they do, but it's piss!

RONNIE: It's not piss. It's packed with antibodies and non-saturated fatty / acids –

ROGER: Give me strength.

RONNIE: It's true! Christian said.

ROGER: 'Christian said'!

RONNIE: It's completely non-allergic, super-rich in iron, / vitamins B and –

ROGER: **Christ that guy gets on my tits.** *(Beat.)*

RONNIE: Furaha's got its own treatment works and a brand new cooling system. I'm going to go find out costs, and put one in here. It could provide another dozen jobs or so, Rog, and we could start buying the stuff these women bring – the word would spread –

ROGER: Damn right the word would spread.

RONNIE: We could send it over in churns to the orphanage fresh every day – we'd have to buy a special vehicle...

ROGER: Yes, we'd have to buy a 'special vehicle' and how much is that going to cost?

RONNIE: It can't be that much! Look, Rog, I told you – even after we've paid off the loans there'll be plenty left for ice creams: this **is** the ice cream!

ROGER: And where exactly do you propose to locate this bloody ice cream factory?

RONNIE: It could only take two acres at the most, a few buildings. We could use that corner up by the ridge, it needs to be near a road. It's genius!

ROGER: No way, Ronnie. No way. I'm not listening to this bullshit. *(He reads.)*

RONNIE: You've been chained to this desk for weeks. *(Beat.)* What happened to my strapping farmer boy?

ROGER: Maybe you imagined him.

RONNIE: What's the matter, Rog?

ROGER: Ach – I'm drowning in this crap. Deeds, leaseholds –

RONNIE: Do you want me to sort it out, darling? You've got enough on your plate.

ROGER: Bloody right. I've got to get the wheat in before the rains. I've got to sack two guys for pilfering fuel. My girlfriend wants to build a bloody ice cream factory on my front drive and my house girl's going in for a caesarean section tomorrow, requiring 60 thousand bob's worth of medical treatment. I'm up to my neck.

RONNIE: Poor boy. *(She puts her arms around him.)* So why don't you leave the financial bumph with me at least. I'm good at that stuff – I actually like it.

ROGER: Thank Christ someone does.

RONNIE: I can take a look at it – along with my dairy plan.

ROGER: You're my mad mad mad mad milk maid. *(He turns to her.)*

RONNIE: Guilty as charged. First time I saw the mountain capped with snow, I thought of mother's milk.

ROGER: Like an enormous tit.

RONNIE: This miracle substance, so unexpected – incongruous – flowing from the epicentre of darkest Africa, luminous, life-giving…like nectar.

ROGER: Sounds to me like Fanta Orange.

RONNIE: You can't stop me, Roger. I'm going to Furaha on Monday.

ROGER: Well at least I'll get some bloody peace.

RONNIE: I have no choice. This is my calling. This is bigger than me. I'm doing it – and nothing – no one – can stop me. *(She exits. ROGER puts his head in his hands. REGINA puts aside her broom.)*

REGINA as SPIRIT: *(Putting aside her broom.)* It is true: she could not stop. And in his bones he knew: Haraka haraka hakuna Baraka. Hurrying hurrying, brings no blessings. It was too fast. *(ROGER looks up, makes brief eye contact with REGINA as SPIRIT, then exits. She strikes the scene and removes her baby bump, assembling a 'bundle' for the next scene.)*

SCENE ELEVEN

REGINA cradles her 'baby', singing softly. ROGER and RONNIE, now heavily pregnant, look on from opposite sides. They do not see or hear each other.

ROGER: Little / Angel.

RONNIE: Little / Angel.

ROGER: So / beautiful.

RONNIE: So / beautiful.

ROGER: My nusu / nusu child. /

RONNIE: *(She turns away.)* My nusu / nusu child. *(Beat.)*

ROGER: *(He turns to REGINA.)* I made a life.

RONNIE: I destroyed a life.

ROGER: Best seed I've ever sown.

RONNIE: Worst thing I've ever done.

ROGER: My brown / baby… /

RONNIE: My brown / baby.

ROGER: I didn't / know.

RONNIE: I / didn't know.

ROGER: I wasn't / sure…

RONNIE: I / wasn't sure…

ROGER: Now I'm / sure.

RONNIE: Now / I'm sure…

ROGER: Now I'm / ready.

RONNIE: Now / I'm ready.

ROGER: Body and Soul.

RONNIE: Body and soul. *(Beat.)*

ROGER: *(He goes to the baby.)* Malaika. I will do anything for you. *(REGINA sees him.)*

REGINA: I believe you will be a good father to this child.

ROGER: I swear to God I will.

REGINA: So she can be sister / for Memsahib's child *(Talking over each other.)*

ROGER: Regina – Sh! Be quiet… /

RONNIE: Roger, she can be / a sister to our child. *(He hears her. Beat.)*

ROGER: Well, yes – *(To them both, awkwardly.)* – in a manner of speaking.

ROGER now hears RONNIE and REGINA, but the women do not hear each other.

REGINA: They will grow / together.

RONNIE: They will / grow together.

ROGER: Yes. I suppose they will. *(Beat.)*

RONNIE: When Regina dies.

REGINA: When I am dead.

ROGER: *(To RONNIE.)* Don't say that. *(To REGINA.)* Don't say that.

RONNIE: Malaika will need / a mother.

REGINA: Malaika / will need a mother.

ROGER: Stop! I can't. I can't think like that.

REGINA: You must.

RONNIE: You must.

ROGER: Must what? *(Beat.)*

REGINA: You must marry her.

RONNIE: Marry me, Roger.

ROGER: Whoa... *(To RONNIE.)* What's the hurry?

REGINA: ⎱You must give our child a family.
RONNIE: ⎰We must give our child a family.

ROGER: Wait! Why? Which child a family?

REGINA: You must arrange this marriage ceremony.

ROGER: Regina, **Shh**...

REGINA: She cannot hear me. But you must hear me.

RONNIE: Marry me, Roger.

ROGER: *(To RONNIE.)* I can't hear you.

REGINA: Or she can take her child away.

ROGER: *(To REGINA.)* I can't hear you.

RONNIE: Roger... Can you / hear me?

ROGER: No. I / can't hear / you.

REGINA: She will go away.

ROGER: *(To REGINA.)* I can't hear you!

REGINA: And she will take away the money. *(Beat.)*

ROGER: The money? *(Beat.)*

RONNIE: Roger! Can you hear me?

ROGER: Yes! *(Beat.)* I can hear you. *(He looks at her.)* Darling,
let's get married.

RONNIE: Darling, I thought you'd never ask.

End of Act One.

ACT TWO

SCENE ONE

REGINA as SPIRIT sits on a hospital bed with a copy of 'Hello' magazine. There is a crib next to the bed containing the 'baby'.

REGINA: Eh heh! Look what I have. It is still here. There is just one magazine in this hospital, it is so dirty and many pages are broken. But this picture it is still here: *(She reads.)* 'Brad Pitt and Angelina Jolie in Africa with their baby, Shiloh.' You know – the first time Bwana Roger brought me to this hospital – to be cleaned from those British – he showed me this picture. He said: 'Look at these people, these are the richest wazungu in the world: they come to Africa to have their babies.' Ayayay! The richest wazungu in the world! Eh heh! They like Africa so much – how can this be? These people wish for their child to be born on African soil because they say 'it is birthplace of all ancestors'. They have travelled to Africa to purchase one orphan girl – and now – you see – they want to come another time in order to purchase one orphan boy to remove to their country. Ayayay! *(Beat.)* And so, you see, I was very happy when my first child was a boy child. Because I knew he would have a very good chance to be selected by these people. *(Beat.)* He did not belong in my village. *(She closes the magazine, gets into bed and peers into the 'cradle'.)*

Also, this name 'Angelina' – tch tch! – I like it very much – it is mzungu word for 'small angel' which is a very good name, even it can bring many blessings. So I have named my daughter with a Kiswahili word – 'Malaika' – meaning also 'small angel'. This is a good name for her. *(Enter ROGER, reading a medical document.)*

ROGER: I knew it – I bloody knew it! Fantastic news, Regina! Listen to this: 'Malaika, has presented HIV-negative on initial DBS polymerase chain reaction testing. If she tests negative again in six weeks then no further treatment is required.'

REGINA: That will be a happy day for me. *(Enter RONNIE.)*

ROGER: Hey, Ron – great news: Malaika's first tests were negative.

RONNIE: Negative? So… Fantastic! That's –

ROGER: And – listen – this is good too: 'As regards Regina's medication, we advise a change of regimen to a new 3-in-1 drug to be taken orally just once a day.'

RONNIE: That's brilliant. So much easier.

ROGER: 'In the meantime, I strongly recommend Regina feeds her baby with formula milk in order to further minimize / risk of transmission.'

RONNIE: No, no, Roger – No, no, that's not right: *(She snatches the document.)* Breast milk is responsible for only a tiny percentage of HIV transmissions, unless the mother is symptomatic, which Regina is not.

ROGER: *(Snatching it back.)* For chrissake shut up about bloody milk. You don't know what you're on about.

RONNIE: Actually, Roger, I've just done a PhD in nutrition and disease – whilst you didn't even manage to finish your poxy course in farming – so, with respect, Malaika's well-being is probably a bit safer in my hands than yours. *(She reaches for the letter, he resists.)*

ROGER: A bit safer? You got to be joking. I don't need a bloody doctorate to know milk from the body of a woman with HIV is more likely to kill a baby than powder from a tin.

RONNIE: Breast milk promotes brain growth / and visual acuity, protects against disease and tailors itself with every feed to the baby's nutritional requirements.

ROGER: 'The **CDC** recommends that HIV-positive women do not breastfeed where safe drinking water and infant formula are available / *(Beat.)* – **as is the case with Regina.**'

RONNIE: Utter crap.

ROGER: It's what's known as 'Doctor's orders.' *(Beat.)*

REGINA: *(In Swahili.)* Milk from a tin is better. *(Beat.)*

ROGER: See?

RONNIE: What does she know? *(Caustically.)* She doesn't even speak English.

ROGER: She knows she'd rather not kill her own baby. *(Beat.)*

RONNIE: What's that supposed to mean?

ROGER: It means –

RONNIE: **What are you suggesting, Roger?**

ROGER: I know / enough about –

RONNIE: How dare you / how dare you how dare you how bloody **DARE** you. *(She exits.)*

ROGER: *(To REGINA.)* What did I say?

REGINA: You said I did not want to kill my baby.

ROGER: What's wrong with that?

REGINA: Nothing is wrong with that.

ROGER: So what's her problem?

REGINA: I cannot say.

ROGER: She's insane! What's the hell's the problem with that woman?

REGINA: I do not know.

ROGER: Jesus… *(He exits in pursuit of RONNIE.)*

REGINA as SPIRIT: *(Striking the scene.)* It was not true. I knew what was the problem with that woman: she had told me. But it was her secret – so how could I tell? This woman was Second Wife. So she was in this family now. And me – I was Mutumia.

She sets for supper.

SCENE TWO

*RONNIE and ROGER are eating supper on the verandah. REGINA waits
on them.*

RONNIE: Saw a lawyer today. About the deeds.

ROGER: Which lawyer?

RONNIE: Guy called Tony Ndegwa. Very charming –

ROGER: **Ndegwa**? Please tell me you're kidding.

RONNIE: Why?

ROGER: Jesus. You really pick them.

RONNIE: He seems very good.

ROGER: Ronnie, he's a bloody baboon.

RONNIE: What's that supposed to mean?

ROGER: Ach, what's the point.

RONNIE: Well he seems highly competent to me. He's
carrying out negotiations to secure all four leaseholds –
making offers the landowners can't refuse – and paying off
the rest so we – at least I – till we're married – own the lot
– lock, stock and barrel. Then he'll get it all tidied up into
one holding company and we're in business.

ROGER: What's wrong with Dr Kapoor's brother?

RONNIE: He's an accountant. Ndegwa's a lawyer.

ROGER: Ndegwa's a bloody ape.

RONNIE: You are disgustingly racist.

ROGER: Racist, how exactly?

RONNIE: Well the words 'ape' and 'baboon' don't carry the
most Aryan of connotations, let's face it.

ROGER: Nor does 'Kapoor'. Piss off, Ronnie, I'm not a bloody
Nazi just because I don't trust Tony Ndegwa. You forget: I
know him. The man's a mkora.

RONNIE: A 'mkora' who just happens to be Kenyan.

ROGER: Yes. And so am I. Ronnie, you forget I've lived and worked with these people – all shades of black, brown, white and everything in between – all my life – all my life – so I know things – about the system – I just – get things that you – that you / – that you

RONNIE: It's not / a 'system' – it's called 'the world'. You 'forget': inter-racial politics is not some sort of secret formula exclusive to the white elite of Africa who've 'lived here all their life' – Dr Kapoor's lived here all his life, Tony Ndegwa's lived here all his life, Regina's lived here / all her life –

ROGER: Yah and they all know a hell of a lot more about living in Kenya than / you do –

RONNIE: It's nothing / to do with living in Kenya – it's called having an open mind.

ROGER: I do have an open bloody mind. But I have an open mind Kenya-style –

RONNIE: Now there's an oxymoron if ever I heard one. Kenya's not some private club –

ROGER: Look – OK – I spend all day every day troubleshooting other people's problems all day, every day, one maneno after another – with my open bloody mind, it's why I'm still here – it's why three hundred people want to work for me and not Tony bloody Ndegwa's father over the hill who invites all his Kikuyu friends to the banquet and starves the rest. That's what you don't understand. *(Beat.)* Believe me, there's a hell of a lot you don't understand about – about – about – but, I'm telling you I'm telling you: you just can't trust these, these, you just don't know where you are with some of these -

RONNIE: **Educated black men.**

ROGER: **Ah, shut up.** You don't know what you're talking about.

RONNIE: **Don't I.** *(Pause. REGINA pours some water for them.)* Regina! My God, what are we thinking, sitting here bickering? My God – Malaika got the final all-clear today! Regina, we should be celebrating. Roger –

ROGER: Yes, I know.

RONNIE: HIV-negative! All clear! It's momentous: Regina, why don't you join us.

(Beat.)

ROGER: She has eaten.

RONNIE: 'She' has, has 'she'?

ROGER: Yes, she ate in the canteen. With the others.

RONNIE: Yes, I know 'she' did. But maybe 'she' might like to join us at our table – for once – instead of waiting on us hand and foot. Because, on this happy day, maybe 'she' might enjoy a little celebration with, say, the woman whose child will be growing up alongside hers – oh and the man who rescued her from those white shits in the first place.

ROGER: Which 'man'? Surely not the racist 'shit' you were talking about a minute ago?

RONNIE: *(Beat.)* It just strikes me Regina might enjoy a little – companionship with some fellow human beings for once. But God forbid we interfere with the apartheid status quo…

ROGER: Hey, you've got it all worked out, haven't you? *(Beat.)* Regina, would you care to join us tonight? We're having a most delightful little soirée? *(Beat.)*

REGINA: Sitaki. *(Beat.) (In Swahili.)* Do you need anything else?

ROGER: Siyo, Regina, yote ni mzuri. We have everything.

(She exits.)

RONNIE: We have everything. And she has nothing.

ROGER: She doesn't have nothing. She has Malaika.

SCENE THREE

ROGER clucks over Malaika, who is cradled by REGINA. ROGER and REGINA are laughing together. RONNIE stands by unobserved, heavily pregnant. She is watching.

REGINA: See she is smiling at you.

ROGER: Are you smiling at me, little girl? Ach, she's a sweetie, man. Malaika – I'm just off to a very big lake to catch you a very big fish!

REGINA: *(Laughing.)* She cannot eat fish! She is too small!

ROGER: *(He sings.)* Malaika, nakupenda Malaika. *(REGINA is amused.)*

RONNIE: *(Approaching.)* You're going to make a lovely Daddy.

ROGER: Hi Ron. You OK?

RONNIE: Not feeling that great actually. Boniface says he's loaded all your gear.

ROGER: What's the matter?

RONNIE: Don't know, bit blah. Might go and lie down. When I've said hallo to this little angel. Habari Malaika? Oh – you smiling at me? What a pretty smile! *(She grimaces.)*

ROGER: Right. Better get on the road, then. *(Beat.)* Are you alright?

RONNIE: God, yeah – I'm fine. Christian and the team from Furaha are here tomorrow to brief me before the Kenya Creameries guys come on Monday.

ROGER: You need to take it easy now.

RONNIE: All this heating and cooling – I swear half the benefits of the raw stuff are lost in the process –

ROGER: Filthy bloody muck.

RONNIE: Pure unadulterated Africa. I couldn't get through the day without my pint of Mama Mziwa special every morning – I'm very faithful.

ROGER: Well it's not doing much for Mama Mziwa – saw her at the gate this morning, looks like she's on her last bloody legs to me.

RONNIE: She should be, poor thing, she collapsed on Friday, miscarriage I think. I took her to the clinic. But she was up and off home next day – twenty Ks across the plateau. The stamina of these women staggers me.

ROGER: Tough as old boots. I saw Father Joseph in town too – you know we've only got a few weeks left to make this toto legal, he needs to see us – together – talk about God and all that for a bit – just to keep him sweet –

RONNIE: Who? Father Joseph or God?

ROGER: Both. It's just a formality. He's keeping Saturday 24th free for us.

RONNIE: That's three weeks.

ROGER: Yah.

RONNIE: I can't – not yet – not with – with the dairy inspection – and everything – Rog, I can't do it that quick.

ROGER: Why not?

RONNIE: Well, you know, whatever it is, invitations, food, drink.

ROGER: I'll arrange it, hey, don't worry about it – ach, I'll put the word out, these rebrobates will come flocking from miles around. It'll be magic.

RONNIE: Well don't do anything just yet.

ROGER: No – but when I get back. We'll go and see him Wednesday.

RONNIE: No, I can't.

ROGER: Why?

RONNIE: I have to go to the clinic. I'm pregnant remember.

ROGER: So I'll meet you at Father Jo's on the way back. What time?

RONNIE: Not Wednesday.

ROGER: When, then?

RONNIE: I don't know. Don't rush me.

ROGER: Don't rush you? You're the one who didn't want a 'little bastard'!

RONNIE: Yeah, well, I know. *(Beat.)* Does it have to be a church-y mzungu affair?

ROGER: Ach, don't let's start this. Look I'll go to any shenzi bloody church you want, OK? We'll dig out our Sunday maridadis and go to the Pentecostal; I'll put on my loin cloth and we'll get the witch doctor in – whatever you like, it's the same bloody result. Ron, let's just do it. While I'm in the mood. *(Beat.)* I love you.

RONNIE: I love you too. *(Beat.)*

ROGER: I want to make an honest woman of you.

RONNIE: Puh! Bit late for that I'm afraid.

ROGER: So let's crack on, hey?

RONNIE: I'm tired. *(She leans on him.)*

ROGER: You sure you're OK?

RONNIE: Don't forget your rod…

ROGER: I won't forget my rod.

RONNIE: Don't forget your flies…

ROGER: I won't forget my flies. *(They laugh. He kisses her and exits. RONNIE grimaces – she is in pain. REGINA watches her intently.)*

RONNIE: Regina, I feel dreadful. *(REGINA goes to speak – but doesn't. Pause.)* You still won't speak to me, will you, Regina? *(Beat.)* **Will you?** Regina. *(She flinches.)* Ow – what is that? *(Beat.)* Regina – is it because you can't speak? Or won't? *(Beat.)* Regina? *(Pause.)* Can't. Or won't. *(Beat.)* He's told you not to, hasn't he? *(She laughs bitterly.)* He's gagged you! The sicko. Do you think he's scared we'll gang up on him, Regina? Not much chance of that – OW… *(She breathes deeply.)* Regina, you know what? Sometimes

I wonder if you have a voice at all. Ow… *(Beat.)* For Godsakes, speak to me, Regina. *(Grimacing.)* Regina, what's happening to me… Aaaaaaaaarrgh…

REGINA: Pole, Memsahib! *(Blackout.)*

RONNIE: Aaaaaaaaaargh – Regina, help me, help me, Regina, help it stop – it's coming – it's too soon – No – NO – NO – Ah-ah-ah-aaaaaaaaaaaaaaaaaah… Regina, help me. **REGINA FOR FUCK'S SAKE DO SOMETHING.**

REGINA: Mama, listen to me now. You must do what I tell you. *(Blackout.)*

SCENE FOUR

RONNIE is on a disheveled, stained bed. REGINA is holding a tiny bundle.

RONNIE: It's no good is it, Regina?

REGINA: It is not so good.

RONNIE: What is it, show me.

REGINA: I think it is not alive. *(She hands it to her.)*

RONNIE: Not alive? It's – oh no oh God oh no – it's – oh no…

REGINA: Pole sana, Mama.

RONNIE: *(Crying.)* NO. No no no no no oh God I'm no good at this. I'm no good at this. Another one… Dead!

REGINA: Next time it will be better.

RONNIE: I don't want a next time, I want this time… Oh my baby, why couldn't you wait we made a pact, we had a pact – you were my baby for Africa… *(She sobs.)*

REGINA: Africa she has very many babies. There will be another.

Malaika stirs, and starts to cry. She gets louder and becomes impossible to ignore.

RONNIE: Malaika – SHUT UP! *(Malaika is quiet for a moment then starts to whimper again. Suddenly –)* Regina, give her to me. I can feed her. *(Beat.)* I can feed Malaika!

REGINA: No, Mama, that is not a good idea – *(Malaika's crying crescendos.)*

RONNIE: Yes, Regina – I can feed her – yes! I've just given birth – I can do it!

REGINA: No, Mama it is not a good idea.

RONNIE: It is a good idea, Regina! It is a good idea! Give her to me. Here, take this one – it's no good – take it away, Regina – put it somewhere – **take it.** *(She hands it to REGINA who swiftly places it on a chair and tries to shield Malaika.)* Give me Malaika. **Regina, give me Malaika.** *(She gets up and takes Malaika roughly from her crib.)*

REGINA: Memsahib, it cannot work. It is not good. *(She tries to take her back.)*

RONNIE: No. No. No… *(The baby's crying subsides as RONNIE nurses it.)* See, she likes it, she likes it Regina – good girl, Malaika, isn't that nice. *(She sings the lullaby.)* 'Malaika, nakupenda Malaika…' Regina, move. I want to see the mountain.

REGINA: Mama she is not your child – you cannot do that – please let me take her –

RONNIE: **Move, Regina. You're in my light.**

REGINA moves behind RONNIE. RONNIE sings quietly, 'Malaika, nakupenda Malaika.' REGINA watches, taut.

RONNIE: There. Now you can see me. She can see me! See, she likes it… See the mountain – I've never seen it so clear. *(Pause as RONNIE experiences an epiphany.)* Once upon a time, Malaika, Mogai, the Lord of Nature, made a big mountain which he called Kere-Nyaga, as a sign of his wonders. He took the man Gikuyu to the top of the mountain of mystery, and showed him the beauty of the country that he, Mogai, had given him. *(Beat.)* Before they parted, Mogai told Gikuyu that, whenever he was in need he should make a sacrifice in the shadow of Kere-Nyaga. *(Beat.)* And the Lord of Nature would come to his assistance. *(Pause.)* It's the Gikuyu legend.

REGINA: I know it.

RONNIE: Yes. I have made a sacrifice today.

REGINA: So next time Mogai can come to your assistance. *(She goes to take Malaika.)*

RONNIE: *(She resists.)* Thank you, Regina. *(There is a palpable standoff which RONNIE wins. Pause.)* I think Mogai already has. *(She coos over the baby.)*

REGINA as SPIRIT: *(Angry.)* Let me tell you. On the day the mother of a Gikuyu child dies, her child is permitted to feed at another woman's breast. Only from that day. But on that day I was not dead. Did you not see: I had assisted that woman with her birth? I had been her teacher: But now, even in her own language, she did not hear.

She roughly removes the stained bedclothes from around RONNIE and covers her with a clean sheet. RONNIE, besotted with the baby, remains oblivious.

SCENE FIVE

Scene as before. RONNIE is still nursing Malaika, singing gently the Swahili song 'Malaika'. REGINA attends. Enter ROGER, fretful.

ROGER: Ronnie, sweetheart – Jesus – are you OK? How – Christ, I'm so – Jesus – I was just – I was just – *(He sees Malaika at her breast.)* Ronnie, what the – ach – No way – **what the hell are you doing?** Suss, no way, stop that, Ronnie – **you can't do that!**

RONNIE: *(Singing.)* Ningekuoa mali we, ningekuoa dada, Nashindwa na mali sina we…

ROGER: Ron, pack it in will you – it's not your baby – suss, man! Let me take her.

RONNIE: *(Still singing.)* Kidege, hukuwaza kidege…

ROGER: Ronnie, give me the baby. *(Beat. She sings.)* **Give me the baby!** *(He grabs it. Pause.)*

REGINA: The baby is mine. Give her to me. *(He looks at REGINA – aghast.)* I am the child's mother. *(He gives her the baby.)*

RONNIE and ROGER look at REGINA, then at each other. RONNIE starts to sob as she fades into darkness. This takes some time. Spotlight on ROGER and REGINA.

ROGER: *(Whispering.)* You spoke…English, Regina.

REGINA: Yes, Bwana.

ROGER: Not Swahili.

REGINA: No. I spoke in English.

ROGER: How long's that been going on?

REGINA: Today it was the first time.

ROGER: Why today?

REGINA: In order to assist Mama with the birth. She required a teacher.

ROGER: I see.

REGINA: English is the language for teaching.

ROGER: Is it? *(Beat.)* Yes I suppose it is. Right. Well, fair enough. Fair enough. But you didn't…you haven't – you didn't mention that I – that Malaika – that Malaika is –

REGINA: Your child.

ROGER: Yes.

REGINA: I did not.

ROGER: Right. Good. *(Beat.)* Well make sure you don't. *(Pause.)* Memsahib will be in hospital for a few days now, Regina, she's very sick –

REGINA: She must not drink this milk.

ROGER: What milk?

REGINA: From that Samburu. Mama Mziwa. It is making her sick.

ROGER: It's certainly making me sick.

REGINA: Veronica she thinks all milk is good.

ROGER: You're not kidding.

REGINA: But some milks are bad.

ROGER: I've told her she shouldn't drink it raw. That stuff is rough.

REGINA: They say Mama Mziwa has a poisonous cow.

ROGER: Who says?

REGINA: Other women who bring the milks. They say the same milk that has poisoned Mama Mziwa also has poisoned Veronica and caused her baby to die in the stomach.

ROGER: Do they, indeed. *(Beat.)* Let me hold her. *(He takes Malaika. They admire her wordlessly together for a moment, smiling.)* Hallo, sweetheart... Jesus. *(Beat.)* I wish I could – I wish I could – I wish I – I – I – *(Beat.)* Have a drink with me, Regina.

REGINA: Just now I must cook.

ROGER: I'm not hungry. What would you like to drink?

REGINA: It is not the custom.

ROGER: What's 'custom'? 'Custom' for who? It's my house. I want a drink – with you. *(She is silent.)* Regina, you're the mother of my child. *(Pause.)*

REGINA: Bwana, she has fed my baby with her breast. She cannot do that again.

ROGER: She won't.

REGINA: I could not stop her.

ROGER: I know. I stopped her. What would you like to drink? *(Beat.)*

REGINA: I would like Fanta Orange.

SCENE SIX

REGINA and ROGER sit on the verandah. She drinks Fanta Orange; he, whisky.

ROGER: Wanjiru.

REGINA: She was Gikuyu.

ROGER: Yes.

REGINA: She was your Ayah.

ROGER: Yes. My Ayah. She looked after me. She was – motherly. Very motherly. To me. My own mother wasn't – didn't – ach – my mother was busy. Running a farm. Four brats. We were wild. She was busy, she had no time. For all that. But Wanjiru – she was – she didn't – think twice, you know, about – holding me, holding me, me holding her. I remember sobbing, sobbing into her – into her – her – her – till there was…nothing. Ach, I was a right little wuss most probably. But I was small. I was only small – two, three, four – just a toto. *(He drains his glass.)*

REGINA: She was a mother to you.

ROGER: Yah. Like a mother. *(Beat.)* Thing is – Regina – you see – I didn't know when to stop. And she didn't stop me. Wanjiru. She never stopped me. Older I got, you know. Four, five, six. I was six that time. That time – my Dad caught me. *(He drinks.)* You see she – Wanjiru – had the most wonderful…most wonderful… Ach, she was very – you know. Generous. You could get lost. I loved the – feel – of her – she was so – so – so – and – and – and so dark. But not black. No. Not, not, not even – brown. Purple. Purple. She was. God, I can – I can – I can – remember. *(He drinks.)* Anyway, I was a dirty little bastard. A filthy little pervert. I used to sneak off to find her. Find Wanjiru. If I was tired. Or pissed off with my brothers. Or I'd been given a slap by my Dad. Any bloody excuse, sneaking off to find her, snuggling in for a – for a – snuffling up for a – for a – a – a – ach. *(He drinks.)* Anyway. One time. My Dad came looking for me. I'd come off my bike, taken the skin off my knees, my brothers were ripping it out of me, ripping it out of me. I ran home. Straight to Wanjiru, who cleaned me up, and let me...let me... And then I – I got right up close – with her – you know – under her – you know – right up close. Like a bloody ferret in a sack. And my Dad walks into the compound – didn't even know he was there till I came up for air – heard his voice. '**What the fuck are you doing you filthy little pervert?**' Nearly shat my pants. *(He drinks.)* Jesus he gave me a hiding. Dragged me off by the ear and beat me till I was blue.

I deserved it. I deserved it. I was ashamed. Still am. Still am. Christ, he was ashamed too – having a pervert for a son. Who can blame him? But he never mentioned it again. I used to think, 'Did that really happen?' Maybe I imagined it. Maybe it was my imagination. It didn't happen. *(He drinks.)* No. It happened. *(He drinks again.)*

Regina, you know what? I don't have to marry her now – do I? The baby's gone. Gone! She can piss off now! I'm sick of her. She's a pain in the arse. With her milk. And her – milk. Bloody...fucking...milk. Christ I'm sick of the sight of her. We're not married yet, Regina – not bloody married yet. Hey? I can get rid of her – rid of her she's got to go. Got to go. *(He drinks. He is by now visibly drunk.)* She can piss off, right? Piss off! I can QUIT. Not doing this any more not doing this **any more.**

REGINA: But what about your farm?

ROGER: What about my farm?

REGINA: Now she is the owner.

ROGER: She bloody isn't. She's outta here – gone! Lucky escape. Kwaheri sana.

REGINA: Now you must marry Veronica or you cannot own your farm.

ROGER: Mustn't. Mussssn't. This farm's in my family for three generations. Fact.

REGINA: All the people they are saying that she is the owner.

ROGER: Bullshit. What people?

REGINA: The chiefs, every other neighbour who owns shambas and lands around about: Bwana Kuldip, Bwana Wilson, Bwana Ndegwa.

ROGER: Ndegwa? He's that bastard lawyer!

REGINA: His family own very much land in this region.

ROGER: Don't you think I know that? Bane of my life – always has been – filthy bloody crook. But I've bought him out. Finally!

REGINA: Bwana, not you – Veronica.

ROGER: No – yes – she coughed up the funds – but the land – the land – the farm – is mine – well ours, maybe. If you want to put it like that.

REGINA: The farm it belongs now to her. This is what the people are saying. All the land, every area. She is the owner. *(He drains his glass and starts laughing manically.)*

ROGER: Bullshit. Sheessnot. *(Beat.)* Regina. I love you. *(Beat.)* Sheeesnott. Snot. *(He laughs.)* Ach, Regina, I quit. I want her out. Achachachach. OUT. *(Long pause. He leans towards her.)* You see Regina? You know what, Regina? You – your skin – your – you – was you – after Wanjiru, the next time I got to touch skin – I loveyourskinregina. *(He laughs.)* Loveit love you Regina you you I found you when you were I found you after they you were there they'd those those bastards…I love you Regina. *(He pours more whisky.)* I want to touch your I love you I love her I love her skin her her I love I…Regina – those bastards how could they those bastards those bastards do that. **That fucking shit**… *(He starts to cry. Lights fade on ROGER.)*

REGINA as SPIRIT: *(To audience.)* I could not breathe. *(Beat.)* Then I became aware there was a man pushing himself on to me, pushing himself into me, it hurt very much, hurt very much. It was my first time, it hurt very much. I tried to lift my head to see his face but I could not, the man who was holding my head he would not allow it. I could hear the men, now there were more men, running on the ground and they were laughing, and making noises, 'Fuck the Bitch Fuck the Bitch Fuck the Bitch!' There were more hands and boots pushing me to the ground. I could not tell how many were using me, it was one, then another then another, all the time I was fighting, and they were chanting: 'Fuck the Bitch'.

SCENE SEVEN

RONNIE, frail in a dressing gown, is drinking tea on the verandah. REGINA is clearing the table. ROGER is pacing up and down with a document.

ROGER: 'Feto-maternal listeriosis'.

RONNIE: Well la-di-bloody da.

ROGER: What did I tell you?

RONNIE: What did you tell me, Roger?

ROGER: I told you: that Samburu muck is rank!

RONNIE: That 'Samburu muck' is pure, natural cow's milk.

ROGER: Precisely. An accident waiting to happen –

RONNIE: On the contrary – it's all subjected to the merciless blasts of pasteurization before anyone's allowed near it. More's the pity.

ROGER: Shenzi bloody moo cows –

RONNIE: Don't you dare demonise my Samburu, Roger, don't you dare –

ROGER: 'Your' Samburu now, are they, Ronnie?

RONNIE: Don't you dare demonise them.

ROGER: I'm not. I'm demonizing their moo cows. Which produced the listeria-riddled crap which killed your baby.

RONNIE: It was also your baby.

ROGER: Yah, well if you ask me it was a lucky escape – *(He reads.)* 'Surviving neonates may suffer infantiseptica and associated physical retardation.'

RONNIE: Can happen to any baby. Where's the proof?

ROGER: 'Bacterial infection which causes intrauterine infection / in pregnant women'–

RONNIE: Blah blah blah blah / blah blah blah blah.

ROGER: 'resulting in / spontaneous abortion or stillbirth in the second and third trimester.' *(Beat.)* I rest my case.

RONNIE: Shut the fuck up Roger. None of this changes the fact that several hundred orphans across the region are now drinking milk every day thanks to an initiative first inspired by my dear Samburu friends. Or that I've just received a massive grant for two state-of-the-art delivery trucks from Detroit –

ROGER: Detroit? That's handy for spare parts.

RONNIE: – and, rest assured, the minute I've got the strength to get my butt off this bloody verandah I'm off to Nyanza to select a second location up / there –

ROGER: For / your –

RONNIE: Yes. For my 'dirt-eaters'. Thought they might enjoy a change of diet. *(Beat.)* So you can stick your 'feto-maternal listeriosis' up your smug-arse little arse. *(Beat.)*

ROGER: You'd better hold your horses. Kenya Creameries have ordered a screening of your entire stock.

RONNIE: Screen all you like. Every batch is double-checked for every nasty imaginable You forget I have had the best advice money can buy. I'm rich. And I'm not stupid –

ROGER: Dr Kapoor is convinced that whatever shit you've been scoffing –

RONNIE: The only 'shit' I've been 'scoffing' is Mama Mziwa's milk. Which never ever made it to dairy. I made damn sure of it: I wanted the real deal. So I kept it for myself. In my fridge. For my baby. *(She exits.)* For Africa.

ROGER: *(Sighing.)* Batty as a fruitcake, Regina. *(REGINA resumes clearing the table.)*

REGINA: She has been to so many schools.

ROGER: Or is it 'nutty'? It's nutty. Regina, leave that. *(She stops.)*

REGINA: Why can she not read the signs? *(He moves next to her.)*

ROGER: Does a fruitcake have nuts? *(He studies her.)* It's OK, Regina, I won't bite. *(He touches her face.)*

REGINA: *(Beat.)* Has she not seen that even dirt from the ground can feed the body? So even milk – a good food – sometimes it can poison the body.

ROGER: She'd be better off with Fanta-bloody-Orange – Regina, what's this on your neck?

REGINA: Why can she not see?

ROGER: It's swollen. There's a swelling. Has Dr Kapoor seen this, Regina? *(Beat.)*

REGINA: He has not.

ROGER: When's your next check-up?

REGINA: It has been this way before. And then it goes away again. It cannot be urgent.

ROGER: You are taking your dawa?

REGINA: I take it.

ROGER: Every day? Every morning? Same time? With food?

REGINA: Many mornings I take it.

ROGER: Many mornings? Regina, what does that mean? It's all about 'adherence' – Remember? Adherence is everything with ARV treatment. You only need to take it once a day. Are you telling me you've been missing days?

REGINA: Each day can be different.

ROGER: **Regina you need to take it at the same time every day.** For chrisssakes. How many times have you missed it?

REGINA: I will take it.

ROGER: How many times?

REGINA: I cannot say.

ROGER: How many times? Once a week? Once a month? How old is Malaika now?

REGINA: Now she is just three months.

ROGER: So how many have you missed? In three months? Would you say?

REGINA: I don't know.

ROGER: More than ten times? *(Beat.)* Regina.

REGINA: I think more than that. I think it is not urgent. These lumps they will go away.

ROGER: *(He takes her face in his hands.)* Regina, you need to see the doctor.

SCENE EIGHT

RONNIE, elated to find MALAIKA unattended, picks her up. REGINA as SPIRIT is in shadow.

RONNIE: Malaika! Habari Malaika! Has she left you all alone? My little angel. I would never leave you all alone. Never. *(Beat.)* I have fed you, my little one, haven't I? Before they could stop me: Malaika had my first milk. *(She whispers.)* They call it 'liquid gold', Malaika: the elixir of life. 'If you give your baby nothing else, make sure you give her this,' they say… And I gave that to you, didn't I? My little angel… *(Enter ROGER.)* Roger! Where have you been? Malaika's all on her own here. Where's Regina?

ROGER: She's coming just now.

RONNIE: I've been talking to AmericAid. They're sponsoring our Nyanza depot!

ROGER: I'm taking her to the clinic.

RONNIE: Aren't you going to congratulate me? I just raised ten thousand dollars to feed my dirt-eaters!

ROGER: Great. Should buy a lot of dirt. Ronnie, do you have a mobile for Tony bloody Ndegwa? He doesn't answer my calls and he's never there.

RONNIE: No. Is Regina OK?

ROGER: No mobile? How do you ever get hold of him?

RONNIE: He can't see you next week: he's in Kisumu with me. Then Nairobi. We'll be gone a while. Weeks, possibly. Is Regina OK?

ROGER: You're going to Kisumu?

RONNIE: We'll be gone a while.

ROGER: With Tony Ndegwa?

RONNIE: She speaks English all the time to me now, have you noticed?

ROGER: You're going with to Kisumu with Tony Ndegwa?

RONNIE: Since the baby... Or non-baby... She actually speaks to me!

ROGER: For how long?

RONNIE: Was that your idea, the English ban?

ROGER: Why are you going with him?

RONNIE: Just an inkling.

ROGER: **Answer me, Ronnie**. *(Pause.)*

RONNIE: Because he's my lawyer.

ROGER: Jesus Christ. He'll be sniffing around you like a dog.

RONNIE: What's the matter with Regina?

ROGER: She's sick. Thought you were building a dairy. Why do you need Ndegwa?

RONNIE: Tony understands the intricacies of Kenyan land law. And I don't.

ROGER: You're not kidding.

RONNIE: What's that supposed to mean?

ROGER: Ron, whose name is on the title deeds for this place now?

RONNIE: Which place?

ROGER: This place. This Farm.

RONNIE: Mine. Why?

ROGER: Why? Because it's my bloody farm, that's why.

RONNIE: Well, yuh...I know what you mean. But technically it's mine now. Technically. I thought you realized that – I showed you all the bumph.

ROGER: What bumph?

RONNIE: All the stuff that came with the sale of the leaseholds, and the mortgage repayments. All that stuff.

ROGER: You waved a few bits of paper at me and got me to sign on some dotted lines!

RONNIE: Yeah, and I showed you the bumph. I said, 'It's all in the small print if you fancy a good read.'

ROGER: 'A bedtime read', you said. And then you seduced me, as I remember.

RONNIE: You didn't seem to object.

ROGER: Hardly likely to.

RONNIE: You could have read it in the morning.

ROGER: It'd gone in the morning.

RONNIE: The Money Fairy is an early riser.

ROGER: The Money Fairy didn't give me a fucking chance.

RONNIE: You could've asked for it back.

ROGER: I thought you were dealing with it!

RONNIE: I was.

ROGER: And I trusted you.

RONNIE: Well there you go then.

ROGER: What do you mean, 'There you go then'?

RONNIE: What do you mean, 'What do you mean?'?

ROGER: Ach, come on, Ronnie, don't play games with me.

RONNIE: Well what do you want to know?

ROGER: What is the situation – 'technically' – with me and this bloody farm?

RONNIE: It's all paid off. No one owes anyone anything. No debts. No mortgage. No leaseholds. All owned. Freehold. Lock, stock and barrel.

ROGER: Owned by who?

RONNIE: 'Whom'.

ROGER: Fuck off.

RONNIE: By me. But with a proviso.

ROGER: What 'proviso'?

RONNIE: That when we marry, legally, it will be jointly owned. By the two of us.

ROGER: *(Pause.)* Right.

RONNIE: Seemed to make sense. To do it that way. Keep it clean.

ROGER: Clean?

RONNIE: Yuh.

ROGER: In what way 'clean'?

RONNIE: Well, you know, keep it in one name. Keep it in the family.

ROGER: Whose family?

RONNIE: Our family. Yours and mine.

ROGER: 'We' haven't got a bloody family.

RONNIE: *(Beat.)* That's cruel.

ROGER: I'm sorry. It wasn't meant to be.

RONNIE: Apology accepted.

ROGER: *(Beat.)* So let's get married! *(REGINA 'enters' the space behind RONNIE. He looks at her. She looks at him. RONNIE does not see.)* Let's get married, Ron.

RONNIE: What's the rush? Don't you trust me?

ROGER: Why are you messing around?

RONNIE: Roger, remind me – why exactly do you want to marry me?

ROGER: Because – because – Oh God. *(He looks past RONNIE at REGINA.)* Because – Oh Christ: because I love you.

RONNIE: Do you?

ROGER: Yes. I do.

RONNIE: Sometimes I wonder.

ROGER: Why?

RONNIE: I don't see it in your eyes any more.

ROGER: *(He looks into REGINA's eyes.)* I do. I love you. You are beautiful and brave, you are loyal and clever and true. You have shown me that love is not where you expect it to be, not where it should be. It is just there. Staring at you. In the face. It is, it is you.

RONNIE: Rog – I – I almost believe you mean that. *(They face each other. ROGER looks at her briefly, walks past her to REGINA and kisses her for a long time. RONNIE exits.)*

ROGER: I can't do it, Regina.

REGINA: She has seen you kiss me like a wife.

ROGER: I don't care. I don't care.

REGINA: She is mzungu. She will not accept another wife.

ROGER: I can't marry her. I'm sorry.

REGINA: What about your farm?

ROGER: I can't do it.

REGINA: What about your child?

ROGER: I can't marry Ronnie. I don't love her. I don't even like her. She's a lunatic.

REGINA: Now everything will be taken.

ROGER: But I love you, Regina.

REGINA: Bwana, I am dying.

ROGER: You mustn't give up hope, Regina.

REGINA: There is no hope now. When swellings come a second time the hope is gone. It is better for the diseases to come quickly so death can come sooner. *(She moves away.)*

ROGER: You've got to try, Regina, you've got to try at least. If not for me then for Malaika. You're a – you're a mother. What about Malaika?

REGINA: Malaika will be very fine. She has a mzungu father. A mzungu cannot be poor.

ROGER: I'm afraid he can.

REGINA: He cannot. A mzungu can always get money from other wazungu. And a house. Malaika will have food. She will have medicines. She will be very fine.

ROGER: I love you Regina. You are…the oracle.

REGINA: It is easy for you to love me. Soon I will go away.

Enter RONNIE with bags.

RONNIE: Ah, Regina there you are: can you ask Boniface to put my bags in Bwana Ndegwa's car. And move the rest of my stuff to your quarters – it's all packed up. And all your stuff should come in here. You are Memsahib now.

ROGER: Ronnie, don't be ridiculous –

RONNIE: Yes, Roger. It makes perfect sense. Regina, you should be Bwana's wife, not me. You are the one he loves – and rightly so: you were here first! I had no business to be here in the first place. I was blind. And selfish. And I'm sorry. Regina. I really am. It should never have happened. But it's OK now – it's easy – we'll just swap! You move in here and I'll move into your place – with Malaika – when I get back. You don't have to worry about Malaika any more. It'll all work out fine. Wish me a good safari. *(She kisses ROGER and REGINA on both cheeks.)* Tell Malaika I'll be back very soon. *(She exits.)*

ROGER: What do we do now, Regina?

REGINA: Now we can do nothing. She has the land. She has the power. Now is too late.

They strike the scene together.

SCENE NINE

RONNIE is driving, singing at the top of her voice, 'Malaika, nakupenda Malaika!'

RONNIE: Aaaaaaaaah! I could sing and sing and sing! My God I haven't felt this – this – **good** – this alive – since – well: ever! Finally, all is right with the world – the Mama Mziwa Depot has found its home on the shores of Lake Victoria, another swathe of African children will imbibe the milk of human kindness – or human guilt – whichever way you look at it. But what does it matter? Nothing matters any more! God I feel good.

Of course I slept with him. Why wouldn't I? He's **so** beautiful… Smart, savvy, kind – knows Africa like the back of his hand – turned up in his own plane out of the blue: my very own 'flying Dutchman'… Of course I slept with him.

Oh, I know, it should've been Tony. Who better than the brilliant Mr Ndegwa with his crisp Saville Row shirt against jet black skin: ought to be every girl's dream. And certainly mine – such divine symmetry: black indigenous male and white immigrant female. Balanced. But, of course, not balanced because Tony sucks his compatriots dry to swell the fortunes of his posse of black elites whilst I will systematically redistribute my land among its rightful owners: the peasant farmers. What am I here in Africa for, after all, if not to give something back?

And I will give something back. I destroyed a life. But then I made my sacrifice. And now I understand why: that child was not meant to be mine, or Roger's. It wasn't ours to have. I misread the signs. How could I miss the one sign staring me so clearly in the face? Malaika, my Malaika – there all along: product of black angel and white devil –

Iam

Iam

Ianm

Iam

Iam

Iam

Iam

fusion of humanity's furthest extremes, yet an empty page: the embodiment of hope. And I fed her. I was there. She is mine. *(She arrives, satisfied.)* Hodi! Roger! Malaika! Anyone home? *(She exits. She enters.)* Where is everyone? *(She strikes her own 'car seat.')*

SCENE TEN

REGINA, semi-conscious, is in a bed. ROGER and RONNIE are there.

RONNIE: Father? What are you talking about? What father?

ROGER: Me. I'm her father. *(Beat.)*

RONNIE: Ah! That's sweet. No. No no. No, Roger. That's sweet but – don't – please: there's no need. I'll take care of her now. Malaika and I share a special bond, you see. She'll want for nothing. It was meant to be. She will be mine.

ROGER: Actually, Ronnie, she's mine.

RONNIE: Roger, don't let's get silly about this. The woman's not dead yet.

ROGER: 'The woman' – Regina – is Malaika's mother. And I am Malaika's father. *(Beat.)* So I will decide what is 'meant to be'. Asante sana.

RONNIE: What the hell are you talking about, Roger?

ROGER: Ronnie, let me tell you something. You may have bought my land, my house, my business, and every drop of blood, sweat and tears my family has shed these past one hundred years, but, as yet, to my knowledge – unless your monkey lawyer can tell me differently – you can't buy genetic parentage.

RONNIE: Shut up, Roger. *(Beat.)* Shut up, Roger. Malaika can't be yours, she's –

ROGER: – mine.

RONNIE: No, she's –

ROGER: – mine.

RONNIE: Malaika is –

ROGER: – mine.

RONNIE: **Don't say that, Roger.**

ROGER: She's mine, Ronnie. Always has been, always will be. *(Beat.)* Regina did have a baby – from the rapes – a year before Malaika. Almost to the day. *(Beat.)* A baby boy. *(Pause.)*

RONNIE: That's not – that's not – No. That's not – / no –

ROGER: Yes. / She left him at her village. She didn't want him, couldn't 'bond' with him you might say, he reminded her of the rapes. So she left him and came to me. And I slept with her, as you know. And made her pregnant – which you didn't know. *(Pause.)* But you do now. Because I'm telling you. *(Long pause.)*

RONNIE: But – so… So… **NO.**

ROGER: Malaika is mine.

RONNIE: Why…but how…but how…but… *(Beat.)* Why didn't you tell me, Roger?

ROGER: I did.

RONNIE: No you didn't. / You didn't –

ROGER: I tried to. / I tried to.

RONNIE: But you didn't.

ROGER: I told you she'd been raped. I told you I'd slept with her. I told you she was pregnant. You jumped to conclusions.

RONNIE: But…you let me.

ROGER: Yes. I let you.

RONNIE: But…no. No. It makes no sense, Roger. It's the wrong ending. *(REGINA stirs.)*

ROGER: Ending for who?

RONNIE: Malaika. Me. Regina. You. Any of us. I figured it out – while I was away – and it all made sense. It's not right, Roger. *(Beat.)* It's not the ending I...I...I wanted.

ROGER: Well it's the ending you're going to get. Sorry, Ron.

REGINA: There is another ending. *(ROGER and RONNIE look at her, surprised.)*

RONNIE: Yes! See! Regina: tell him, tell Bwana: I'll take her; I'll take Malaika. I fed her. I was there! It makes perfect sense. You see that, Regina, don't you?

REGINA: I do not see that. But there is another ending.

RONNIE: No, Regina. Please. Don't. Please don't. You're dying.

REGINA: You can be Mama if you want.

RONNIE: Yes, Regina, I can! See, Roger – I can!

ROGER: Regina, she can't. No way. It's the one thing her money can't buy. She can't.

REGINA: Bwana, it is possible for her to buy one child. With money. It is possible. You remember those wazungu from that magazine? The richest in the world?

RONNIE: Which wazungu? What magazine?

ROGER: Hah! Yes. Yes... Brad Pitt and Angelina Jolie.

REGINA: These people: they came to Africa from United States America to take a girl child. They will return to purchase a boy.

RONNIE: You have a boy...

REGINA: I have a boy. He is in my village. My sister she is waiting for these two people to come and buy him for very much money, maybe even one thousand dollars US – very very much money. But even you have much money – it is the same. It can be you.

RONNIE: I'll give your sister anything, Regina –

REGINA: It is good. Then she can buy uniform to go to school. A roof for my grandmother's house. Even an iPod. But do not tell her you have seen me. My sister she has not seen this magazine, she cannot recognise these people. You must tell her that you are these people. She will not know.

RONNIE: Roger, will you come with me?

REGINA: He will go. You will go together. But the child it can be yours, Mama.

RONNIE: Mama. Me. My nusu nusu child. A boy. *(Beat.)* What's his name, Regina?

REGINA: His name is Brad.

SCENE ELEVEN

ROGER and RONNIE are in an African village, huddled in a corner. REGINA as SPIRIT is in shadow.

RONNIE: He's black.

ROGER: Yes.

RONNIE: He's not brown.

ROGER: No.

RONNIE: He should be brown.

ROGER: Well, he's brown-ish.

RONNIE: He's brownish-black. He should be brownish-white.

ROGER: He's dark brown. *(Beat.)* Very dark brown.

RONNIE: He's black.

ROGER: He's black-ish.

RONNIE: He should be light brown.

ROGER: Maybe in the sunlight…

RONNIE: Milky. Like Mailaika.

ROGER: You could give him a shower…

RONNIE: He should be nusu nusu.

ROGER: He is nusu nusu.

RONNIE: He isn't.

ROGER: He is. Nusu British, nusu Kenyan.

RONNIE: But he isn't. He's jet black. And…and…he's…he's… He's not…nice. He's covered in flies. His eyes are gammy, there's green snot running down his…and his legs are all …I mean – **what is that**? He's all rough and scaly. And he smells.

ROGER: They might be a bit low on shower gel.

RONNIE: But – No. He looks…wrong. And he looks…hostile. Angry. He's the wrong one, Roger. He's the wrong one. They're trying to give me the wrong one!

ROGER: Well they're not going to give you another one.

RONNIE: What do I do?

ROGER: You could paint him.

RONNIE: Do you think they're hiding him? Will you ask?

ROGER: No, I won't bloody ask. What do you expect me to say, 'Have you got a better one? A browner one, with a bit less snot?'

RONNIE: It can't be him.

ROGER: It is him. It's Brad.

RONNIE: But, Roger – he can't be.

ROGER: He can be.

RONNIE: Roger, he can't.

ROGER: He can, Ronnie.

RONNIE: How can he?

ROGER: If his father was black.

RONNIE: If his father was black?

ROGER: Yes.

RONNIE: You mean, if Regina had someone else – before the –

ROGER: No. I don't mean that.

RONNIE: Well he can't be one of the soldiers' –

ROGER: Yes he can.

RONNIE: He can't, Roger –

ROGER: He can. There was one.

RONNIE: One what?

ROGER: One soldier. I remember now. One of the soldiers was black.

SCENE TWELVE

REGINA as SPIRIT sits up in bed, brightly lit. ROGER and RONNIE are at her side.

REGINA as SPIRIT: *(Chanting.)* 'Fuck the Bitch.' *(Beat.)* Soon my head was swimming as if in water and I could not fight any more. Then it became quiet, there was only one man remaining, the same one who had been holding my head. Now I could see him. He went to the other end of me and he gave sex to me. It was quiet. Now I could not fight – but I could see him. I could hear him, 'OK, Sister, my turn now.' Then when he had finished he said, 'Thanks, Sister. *(Beat.)* Bitch. *(Beat.)* Happy new year.' And then he returned to the car. It was so strange. It was so strange. Because, this man, he had the voice of a mzungu. *(Beat.)* But he was black. Like an African.

> *Stillness. RONNIE folds REGINA's arms on her chest. ROGER closes her eyes, kisses her mouth and pulls a sheet over her head. ROGER and RONNIE strike the scene.*

SCENE THIRTEEN

RONNIE and ROGER are either side of REGINA's grave. REGINA as SPIRIT can be seen in shadows, watching them. They do not see her.

RONNIE: I took him, Regina. I hope you know that.

ROGER: I made damn sure of it.

RONNIE: I'd have taken him anyway. *(Beat.)* He's just not what I – what I was – expecting. That's all.

ROGER: Black as the ace of spades.

RONNIE: It's not funny, Roger.

ROGER: It's not meant to be.

RONNIE: No. Well it's not. He's HIV-positive, Regina. It's
not funny being born with a death sentence. It's not
funny to never feel that spring in your step that is every
child's birthright. And he knows. That look in his eye –
all-knowing – like you, Regina. He knows his days are
numbered, knows he was born condemned, unwanted.
(Beat.) Unloved.

ROGER: What's to love? Miserable little bugger.

RONNIE: Shut up, Roger. *(Beat.)* Look. Regina, I can't lie –
he is hard to love: the way he looks at me – at everyone,
if you could see him, as if he doesn't want to love, or be
loved. He's…unloveable. At least, very hard to love. But
I'm trying, Regina, God I am trying. It's ugly, frustrating,
it's pretty thankless to be honest. It's a real – a real
sacrifice. But that's what I came to Africa for. But, you
know all that, Regina – you of all – it was you who figured
it out. And you were right. Brad is Africa's ending. For me.
(Beat.)

ROGER: 'Africa's ending.' Jesus. Hear that, Regina? Africa's
bloody endings. So see if you can 'figure' out Africa's
ending' for me? Farm Manager I am now. You were right:
it's all hers now. I rent my own house for me and Malaika.
Like a bloody squatter. Like a bloody – Kikuyu. *(Beat.)*
And 'Memsahib' has built a shenzi bloody place bang next
door where she knocks about with the delightful 'Brad' and
her goddamn milkman. Jesus. *(Beat.)* But what choice do
I have, Regina? Tell me. I couldn't marry her – could I?
(Beat.) Christ, I'd rather be poor.

RONNIE: Hardly 'poor', Roger, when there's people –

ROGER: **Shut the fuck up**. Ronnie. Has it escaped your
notice that all these so-called shambas you're flogging to
all these – these – **vultures** – are wrecking this joint before
our very eyes: soon nothing will grow. Ach, Regina, this
place – you should see it: chickens, mangy bloody dogs,
rusty old Kimbo cans all over the place, open drains – I

can't move – how the hell am I supposed to 'manage' a farm over-run with bloody junglies trying to grow bananas and beans on the same bush? It's a fucking joke.

RONNIE: It's called subsistence farming.

ROGER: **Don't you tell me about farming**. Ach, you know what, Regina? *(Beat.)* I knew she was one of those: minute we met. Spot them a mile off: geophagy, milk, orphans: yak yak yak. And what will happen to those poor buggers when the Yanks find a better idea and pull the plug? Or 'Memsahib' gets bored and decides to head home to 'Shropshire'?

RONNIE: That's not going to happen, Roger – I've made a commitment to Kenya.

ROGER: 'Commitment to Kenya.' Two years, Regina, couple of ice cream shops, and she's made a 'commitment to Kenya.' Jesus, Ronnie, you just don't get it, do you? You can't just turn up in a place and know every bloody thing – there's – there's **layers**, man – **layers** – **things** underneath you can't – you can't – see, can't know – until – until you've put in the bloody **time**.

RONNIE: **Time.** Here we go. Your answer to everything, isn't it, Roger? No point even –

ROGER: **Yes.** It is. Ronnie. And it's the one thing you can't offer. Time. Years. Generations. There is no substitute. It might not be the way things 'should' be but it's the way they are. Or were, Regina, till she came along. Bloody do-gooding mzungu with her 'Africa's endings'. Jesus. *(Beat.)* Anyhow, she's not my ending – thank Christ.

RONNIE: **Touché.** *(Pause.) They both look at the grave.*

ROGER: No. *(Beat.)* There was only ever one woman for me – ever. And her name was – well, Regina, you know what her name was. *(Beat.)*

REGINA as SPIRIT: Her name was Wanjiru. *(They hear her but do not see her.)*

ROGER: Yes. *(Beat.)* Wanjiru.

RONNIE: Wanjiru?

ROGER: My Mother.

RONNIE: She was your Ayah.

ROGER: She loved me. I loved her. *(Beat.)* She was my Mother.

RONNIE: She wasn't your 'mother', Roger –

ROGER: What makes you so sure?

RONNIE: Because she – well! I mean – she was…she was…

REGINA as SPIRIT: She was black. *(The light changes.)*

RONNIE: Yes. *(Tentative.)* She was black.

ROGER: Yes. *(Defiant.)* She was black. *(Beat.)*

REGINA as SPIRIT: So – can you see? *(They listen.)*

RONNIE: See – what? *(The light intensifies.)*

ROGER: See what… Regina? *(They are listening hard.)*

REGINA: Wanjiru was black. You are white. You were both Africans. And she was a mother for you.

RONNIE: But – No.

ROGER: Yes.

REGINA: And you, Memsahib, you are white. Brad is black. You are both British. And you are a mother to him.

ROGER: So – No.

RONNIE: Yes.

REGINA: So – it can be this way. *(Beat.)*

ROGER: But –

RONNIE: But –

REGINA: But Malaika – she is black and white in one. She is mixed.

ROGER: Yes.

RONNIE: Yes.

REGINA: Yes. *(Beat.)* So can you see? *(They strain to see her.)*

RONNIE: No. *(Beat.)* Yes…

ROGER: Yes. *(Beat.)* No…

REGINA: Many times now a thing is so clear. Many times it is mixed up. It is nusu nusu. So it can be this way. *(The light mutates to a half light. Silence.)*

RONNIE: Can you see her?

ROGER: Sort of. Can you?

RONNIE: Yes. And No. Can you hear her?

ROGER: Yes. She spoke.

RONNIE: 'Can you see?' she said.

ROGER: Yes. *(Beat.)* Can you?

RONNIE: I don't know. *(Pause.)* Can you? *(They both squint into the darkness.)*

ROGER: No. Yes. Well…no and yes.

RONNIE: Yes and no.

ROGER: Like she said.

RONNIE: Nusu Nusu.

ROGER: That's what she said.

RONNIE: *(Beat.)* Regina? *(Beat.)*

ROGER: Regina are you there? *(Pause.)*

REGINA as SPIRIT: If you see me then I am here. *(Beat.)* It is just another way to see.

The End.